10-17-94

———————— *A New Day* ————————

A New Day
Anita Bryant

BROADMAN PRESS
NASHVILLE, TENNESSEE

All Scripture quotations are from the *King James Version of the Bible* unless otherwise stated.

Scripture quotations marked NASB are from the *New American Standard Bible.* © The Lockman Foundation, 1960, 1962, 1963, 1968, 1971, 1972, 1973, 1975, 1977. Used by permission.

Library of Congress Cataloging-in-Publication Data

Bryant, Anita.
    A new day / Anita Bryant.
        p.   cm.
    ISBN 0-8054-5352-0
    1. Bryant, Anita.   2. Singers—United States—Biography.   3. Christian biography—United States.   I. Title.
ML420.B84A3   1992
782.42164'092—dc20
    [B]   91-37477
                                          CIP
                                          MN

In loving memory of
my Dad, Warren G. Bryant

January 20, 1921   _August 4, 1991_

When Dad taught me gardening, he
was really showing me how to take the
garbage of life and turn it into
compost—then as the soil combines
with God's sun and rain, it produces a
beautiful and life-giving garden to
sustain not only ourselves but our
neighbors. May the suffering of my
life be used to comfort others and to
glorify our Heavenly Father.

—Anita Jane Bryant

Contents

Acknowledgments . . . ix

Introduction . . . xiii

1. God, How Can I Possibly Forgive? . . . 19

2. Lord, Help Me Handle My Fears . . . 32

3. Meeting That Strange Woman—Myself! . . . 44

4. My Family—My Fortress . . . 52

5. My Amazing Kids . . . 62

6. Friends and Other Angels . . . 79

7. Making New Moves . . . 90

8. The Business of Business . . . 103

9. Money and Prosperity . . . 129

10. By the Grace of God . . . 139

11. Because I Really Need You . . . 157

12. To Love Again . . . 168

13. Home to My Roots . . . 180

14. It's a New Day . . . 196

Acknowledgments

It is impossible for me to remember every person who has made a significant difference in my life during the last eleven years. If you happen to be one of those I have forgotten to mention, please know from the bottom of my heart that without you touching my life with your love and kindness, I never would have seen a new day.

Thanks to:

. . . Charlie, my childhood sweetheart. You've read the last chapter of *A New Day,* but please read the rest. I believe it will be as healing for you to read it as it was for me to write it! Thanks for being my husband, my lover, but most of all, my friend.

. . . my precious children who have endured the storm and have grown stronger through adversity.

In relinquishing you, *Bobby,* you perhaps had it hardest of all, but in the pain, as you pressed on through, found yourself a strong child of God, a gifted writer, and the beginning of a deep and abiding friendship with your mom.

Gloria—watching your struggle through fear, confusion, and suppressed anger almost did me in, for I was helpless to do anything for you, but your struggle gave you strength. The Lord brought you through that dark valley with a light in your heart to help others through social work. We became real friends, and God worked a healing in us together.

Billy, you seem to have ridden the storm easier than anyone, and I believe you stayed in the eye of the hurricane, which amid the storm has a calm area twenty miles in circumference! That eye is Jesus in our spiritual life, whom you trusted as Savior when you were a very small child. God has been faithful and has given you a rare gift in your art to show beauty to an ugly world.

Barbara, those difficult years following the divorce, as each child flew from the nest, found the two of us at home together. Being so much alike in personality and singing ability, we more often than not collided in our frustration to work out our individual problems. I could only go to the Lord and put you on the altar. How faithful our Heavenly Father has been to both of us. When you finally flew from the nest, really on your own, I wept like a baby. On your every return trip home, we are becoming better friends. It's not only a new day for me but for you as well—as you soon finish college with high marks and the ability to soar higher than your mom ever dreamed of, once you decide where you want to fly. . . .

. . . to Charlotte Hale (Pinder) from the beginning, starting with *Mine Eyes Have Seen the Glory,* who for most of my past ten books and this one has gathered the information and has creatively put it into the proper form for public readership. Thanks, my gifted sister, for your ability to convey my words and heart to the reader. Most of all, thanks for the many times in my wilderness journey you always made time for listening to my heart's cry and then responded with love, wisdom, and an encouraging word. . . .

. . . Mama and Daddy (Paw Paw) George—I knew you would, but thank you for always being there for me, loving me, listening to me, giving me the space to find my own answers, lending me money when I was desperate, and most of all for nurturing my children when I was helpless. I love you. . . .

. . . my sister Sandra and her husband, Sam Page, and my nieces, Kathy, Lisa, and Michelle, who were there for me at every turn . . .

. . . Jewel, a friend who listened and cared. . . .

. . . Svea Green (Farmor) for all your years of caring for the children; these past years have not been easy for you either, but thank you for becoming my friend . . .

. . . Broadman Press for believing in me, for its witness and living out daily in its business a commitment to Christ and His excellence.

Love,

Anita Bryant

Introduction

This is the book I said I'd never write. Its contents have been eleven painful, yet triumphant, years in living and learning. It concerns a woman—only one among hundreds of thousands of others like her today—whose life nearly became cut off by forces beyond her control.

The real trials of that desperate time—hard-fought battles with fear, need, loneliness, anxiety, estrangement, alienation, failure—preoccupy and deplete far too many of the individuals you and I know.

Such devastation, even outright cruelty, has become commonplace in today's world. Sadly, often the same spouse who vowed to love, honor, and cherish their mate, eventually becomes the instrument of that mate's downfall.

Nor does one's age guarantee a person much security these days. Dumping an aging wife scarcely rates a raised eyebrow in our cynical society. At the other end of the age spectrum, we staff low-paid office, restaurant, and other service jobs with women in their teens and twenties, divorced or never married, who already are trapped in failure cycles even before they look much older than the babies wailing for their attention.

For me, devastation occurred in 1980 when I was forty. The wipe-out felt paralyzingly swift, complete, and final. After all, when a nationally-organized, thoroughly politicized movement aims to bring down one person, announces boycotts, issues bodily threats, and publicly dares anyone to hire that individual, even the most thriving career will vanish faster than a snowball in the Sahara Desert.

People all over the nation have asked, "Whatever happened to Anita?" Maybe you have an idea—perhaps not. In 1977 our family was being blessed beyond one's wildest expectations. Bob Green, then my husband and manager, and our four children were living in Miami Beach, Florida, not only as a home but as a base for my highly productive career.

We were deeply involved in our church, and our pastor informed the congregation that the Dade County Commission was going to pass a law which would favor homosexuals in the county to have the so-called "right" to teach, even in private religious schools. Our pastor and other church members encouraged me to take a public stand against the proposed new law. Later we were joined by many other preachers, priests, and rabbis. All races and religions were united once they learned the true facts concerning the ordinance.

Bob and I felt it was a local issue, although we learned much later it was of a far broader scope. In fact, at the same time, a national homosexual bill, HR2998, had been introduced in Congress. Because of my Christian convictions, I made my stand—not against homosexuals as persons but against legislation that would tend to "normalize" and abet their life-style, and would especially afford them influence over our children who attended private religious schools. I testified along with others against the legislation before the Dade County Commission. The commissioners were already committed to passing it anyway—and did. At first I did not want to become involved but forged ahead since many encouraged me in my public stance for a Christian view of home and family, and protection of our children. I was asked to lead a referendum so we formed "Save Our Children" to change that unconstitutional, unnecessary law. The gay rights law was voted down by the people, not once but three years in a row.

Through the media the referendum had become a national spectacle with me in the middle. I was soon called "too controversial," and opposition to me snowballed to the extent that my sponsors, including a lucrative contract for my own TV show and the Florida Citrus Commission, were finally pressured into dropping me as their spokeswoman.

The attendant stresses and strains on our family finally precipitated my summer 1980 divorce from Bob, a calamity I previously thought impossible.

(Three of the children stayed with me, and the oldest chose to live with his dad and finish his senior year in high school. Then came a series of moves—first back to Oklahoma in May of 1980 for eleven months; then to Selma, Alabama, for three years from June 1981 to June 1984; with my two oldest children in college then, the twins and I in August of 1984 shuffled off to Atlanta, where we remained five years; when the twins went off to college, I made a career move to Nashville, Tennessee, [August, 1989]. After being single ten years, I married former Astronaut Test Crewman Charlie Dry, who had been a childhood sweetheart. We moved to Berryville, Arkansas, near Eureka Springs, on March 1, 1991, where Charlie and I opened the "Anita Bryant Show" in May of 1991.)

But for Anita Bryant what happened then? *After* you're forced into retirement at forty, with four kids to support? *After* the divorce? *After* the sensationalism and blacklisting? *After* rejection, late-night talk-show ridicule, even a pie in the face?

That's why this book is written. My purpose is *not* to catalog and rehash my own personal injuries, insults, and injustices (only a loser dwells on misfortunes years after they happen!) but to record God's redemptive uses of our most grievous tribulations. The good news wins out *every time*. When disaster strikes your life or mine—or that of your pastor, neighbor, parent, son, or daughter—God stands fast. The world may seem to sway and shift beneath your feet. Friends may desert you. Strangers may judge, curse, or abuse you. Even Christians may at best misunderstand, or judge you, and at worst actually become malicious.

Nevertheless, I'm here to tell you from firsthand experience: you are not alone. Despite the most horrifying or hopeless circumstances, you need not be washed up, finished, or beyond hope. God is there, even when you cannot pray and desire not to pray. He knew your name before the foundation of the world. He holds your life in His eternal hands, and He will not let you fall. I know.

Eleven years ago, amid the spectacular wreckage of my life, viewed before the whole world, my mind *knew* these things. At the same time, however, for the first time in my experience, my mind also knew deep depression, fear, suicidal thoughts, anxiety, and grief. I had said I'd never divorce and when it occurred, I felt self-hatred in all its force, and with it the negative conviction that never, never, *never* could God ever restore the mess my life had become.

How does anyone emerge intact from such hopelessness? This book will show the faithfulness of our God, who from the chaos and wreckage of His children's lives can build something magnificent! Men's evil intentions could succeed in *temporarily* destroying my career, but what people meant for evil, God has used for good. I was to learn the unspeakable depths of God's richest love toward Anita Bryant—and *you*—not because of successful careers, fame, or fortune or any other such temporal thing, but that *His love for His child surpasses all else in life and stands throughout eternity*.

Introduction

Though much of this story is mine, it also is yours. Each of us must discover God's triumphant, tender, and redemptive power in our own lives. Often these discoveries grow out of the worst chapters of our lives, for only then will we draw close enough to Him to appropriate His sublime healing and His amazing grace.

We find that love and grace at the foot of the cross.

1

God, How Can I Possibly Forgive?

That miserably hot day in July 1980, I was aware I'd reached bottom. For weeks my divorce had been splashed onto newspapers, magazines, and supermarket tabloids. We were still making our home in Florida where we had lived since 1960. I encountered myself everywhere: on the television, on the radio, even in a magazine I skimmed through while waiting outside a pastor's study.

Friends had urged me to consult a pastor-counselor in another city. I didn't know him personally, but I respected his reputation. He seemed glad to see me, greeting me warmly and then asking his secretary to serve me coffee or a soda. When I declined, he immediately launched into an intense sermon aimed at me. I listened, mostly in silence, and occasionally I answered a question. When at last he finished I left, almost running, for the ladies' room and exploded into tears.

Condemnation! That episode was to become a pattern in my life. The counselor knew what he'd learned about me only from the media, I realized, splashing cold water onto my face to bring the tears under control. I admired his zeal and his hatred of divorce, but did he have to remind me that I'd been married to a professed Christian man for twenty years, had four wonderful children, and enjoyed a high profile as a Christian entertainer? Did he really suppose I could forget for even one minute?

Why had he assumed I took divorce lightly? Couldn't

he see my agony? I felt anger and despair rise within me, as tears gushed from my eyes. I believed that the factors leading to my divorce belonged to God and me alone. I owed no one else an explanation. Even if my humiliation must be public, I passionately felt I had the right to keep private the most painful and personal details of my life. My main concern was to protect my children, and I wouldn't try to justify myself to this pastor or to anyone else!

Struggling to regain a measure of calm, I felt fury and rage begin to build within me. My hostility extended to every nosy, self-righteous person who wrote me, telephoned me, or stopped me on the street to protest my divorce, demand that I explain it, or quote Scriptures out of context to me. I expected no applause for what had happened, but neither did I expect strangers to confront me in the grocery store, informing me that they'd never pray for me again.

A few hours later I sat in a serene parlor at the home of my friends, John and Bobbie Ames, in Selma, Alabama. I fled to Bobbie because there seemed no better place to go. In that tiny town, graced with Victorian houses and old-fashioned manners, Bobbie reigned as a true Christian lady—a friend who could love unconditionally her younger, shattered sister in Christ.

Here was a place of dignity, respect, and love. Slowly my wound-up emotions began to rest as Bobbie ministered to me with food, tall glasses of iced tea, and quiet conversation. When we retired to her parlor, though, Bobbie's ministry began in earnest.

"Bob's behaving like a madman," I told her, describing my problems with a newly divorced husband who, for some reason, wasn't going along quietly with the fact that our four children would live with me.

"He hurts, Anita. He needs a lot of love right now."

"Yeah? Well, what about me? I hurt, too, but who

cares? I'm exhausted. I don't have a husband, a job, or a home. I don't know where to go from here."

At this, Bobbie interrupted me. Gently but authoritatively, she dropped her bombshell. "You go to your knees. We're going to ask God to forgive you for your sins against Bob, and ask Him to help you forgive Bob for his sins and for everything he ever did to hurt you. It's time for God to lead you to a place of forgiveness."

I simply stared. *Forgive? Someday, maybe. Eventually, I guess.* After all, I realized what God says about forgiveness. "But I can't right now," I blurted out. "I can't!"

"You must," Bobbie said firmly. "You need to begin your forgiveness process today. Later you'll ask Bob to forgive you for any wrongs you've committed against him."

I felt trapped. I simply couldn't believe that Bobbie expected me to do anything of the sort. She understood some of the recent events of our lives, though she never commented or interfered. *This,* I thought, *was just going too far!*

"You must," she repeated. "Whether or not you two ever can be reconciled—and only God knows that— there's still the fact of your children. God gave those kids *two* good parents, in spite of both of your failings in the marriage. Unless you forgive Bob, you'll begin to isolate them from their father, and that will only result in hurting the children. I know from your own painful childhood that you don't want that to happen to them. Although, as you have shared with me, there was a tremendous void when it came to intimacy in your relationship with Bob, he loves those kids.

"You need to build a workable relationship with Bob, and he with you, for your children's good. God expects you to be willing to try, Anita. Just try to forgive Bob, and the rest will follow."

Bobbie Ames took my hands in hers, then asked God to lead me. Quivering, I confessed my willingness to be willing to forgive. At last I raised my wet face and released a deep sigh. For the first time in months, I felt peace steal into my spirit. My tired soul began to rest, and at that moment I realized that something new was about to happen. The road was making a U-turn, and I was headed toward healing.

There would be miles and miles to go, but I had taken that significant first step.

Why We Must Forgive

When God guided me toward a righteous friend that day, I believe He saved me months, perhaps years, of anguish. Oh, that didn't mean the debris of the past wouldn't be brought up time after time but, once you've been to the foot of the cross, at least you recognize where to leave your unforgiveness. Unfortunately, all around us these days we see victims of this bondage—men and women who choose not to forgive. They dedicate themselves to holding other people's sins and faults against them as fresh as the day they happened.

These voluntary victims stay emotionally stuck in the same old grooves; the needle plays their worn-out complaints again and again, while life passes them by. Perhaps you know someone whose spouse left her or him for another person. Years later, alone and bitter, the victim can still recite the former spouse's wrongs as though they had happened yesterday. This bitter cup has been allowed to become the victim's litany and life. They think nothing can replace them.

Although my circumstances were different, that could have been my story, had Bobbie Ames not pushed me into obeying the Lord's very plain injunction: "Forgive us our [trespasses] as we forgive [those who trespass against us]" (Matt. 6:12).

I didn't feel like praying that prayer, yet nothing positive can happen until we pray about it and try to mean it.

God's instructions work. The forgiveness He requires really is our starting place.

Thank God for Bobbie's tough love. Even if you're not used to praying—or never before have approached God, or don't want to pray—you can do it now. He is there. When you confess your sins and then ask Him to help you forgive anyone who has sinned against you, a miracle will happen. God will help you take that step.

Even as I prayed against my will, in my heart I knew the decision was right and would point me toward healing. Why? Because it's important to act from faith and obedience, rather than from fractured feelings. He honors our obedience every time! A wounded spirit will find it very difficult to obey the Lord's leading, especially if hurts were inflicted by other Christians, but, only by yielding our "rights to ourselves" to God, is it possible to let go of our stored-up bitterness and venom.

Forgiving other people gradually became easier and easier to do, but forgiving myself seemed impossible. All my life when any problem occurred, I always took it upon myself to fix it, even though I was only *part* of the problem. I felt almost criminally responsible for my failings toward God, my children, my ministry, my family . . . and on and on and on. Those strong feelings produced frightening physical symptoms—loss of appetite, insomnia, choking on food, chest pains, shortness of breath, and feelings of suffocation and depression.

Wherever my tortured mind happened to linger, I had failed someone, and when I tried to pray about the problem I became filled with self-loathing.

I had hurt so many people! *Never,* I reasoned, *could this mess be straightened out. If everyone hated me, I understood why. After all, I hated myself, too. How could I possibly love myself? How could God love me?*

For me, self-forgiveness would require long, tedious work. Eventually I would come to realize that I, like so many other American women, suffered terribly from low self-esteem. As Anita Bryant the singer, I'd spent my life working hard to earn the love, approval, and applause of others. But *that* Anita Bryant no longer existed.

Now I found myself stuck with plain Anita Jane—forty, divorced, scared, and failing. This woman deserved no applause. Frankly, I held her in contempt.

I had discovered that women often find it impossible to forgive themselves, especially if it relates to a man; and well-disguised low self-esteem may be the root of the problem. Whether or not you believe in God, His principles still operate. Since the fall of mankind in the garden of Eden, as God spoke to Eve, "thy desire shall be to thy husband, and he shall rule over thee" (Gen. 3:16), then nothing else (except in Christ) can fulfill a woman if she has blown it with the man in her life. No matter what you do as a woman, at an emotional level there is still that gnawing inner feeling that you are a second-class citizen if you do not have a man in your life. Likewise most men are operating under God's declaration: (vv. 17-18) "Cursed is the ground for thy sake; in sorrow shalt thou eat of it all the days of thy life; Thorns also and thistles shall it bring forth to thee." Therefore, a lot of men, if they are not wholeheartedly following the Lord by rejecting the old law of sin and walking with a new spirit, are *more* concerned with making a living than with cultivating personal relationships. Only true liberation in Christ can free men and women from the emotional and spiritual results of the curse.

Can God really heal problems so tangled, those we scarcely even recognize in ourselves, much less isolate or find the courage to deal with?

Yes, He can. For me, the process proved often agonizingly slow and painful. The Lord had a purpose for Anita Jane, and He wasn't necessarily in a hurry, though there was much work to do. From the beginning I realized the fundamental need for self-forgiveness, but the sin of procrastination prolonged the process for quite some time. The alternative, though, was torment.

God provided certain godly individuals whose training and skills helped me gain the insights and healings my wounded spirit so desperately needed. Along the way many others like Dr. Paul Walker, pastor of Mount Paran Church of God in Atlanta, Georgia, came to my aid. He has a Ph.D. in psychology with counseling skills, but he lines it up with God's Word to help change a person's life. I could fill these pages with many others who provided the special word, encouragement, or scriptural principle at exactly the moment I needed it most.

And then, to show me an unforgettable portrait of self-forgiveness, God sent me to Ken Simmons.

Propped high against a mound of pillows in his narrow hospital bed far down the corridor of an Atlanta hospital, Ken's thin, young face at first looked whiter than the linens behind it. His bony fingers stretched toward me, and his eyes, large and luminous, appeared to sparkle with pleasure as I approached. All the life in his body seemed to pour through those eyes.

The hospital required our scrubbing up before visiting, and I tried not to show my nervousness. Ken, a friend of my friend Russell McCraw, had AIDS. Russell had helped lead Ken back to the Lord as he had so many others trapped in a homosexual life-style. I had come to pray with Ken and share some Scriptures concerning healing. I had oil with which to anoint him and the hope that we would see a miracle from God.

"I pray he's not too sick to see you," Russell had said. "He's so ill."

Little did I dream that this thirty-two-year-old man, who looked as young and handsome as my sons Bobby and Billy, would minister to *me*.

Ken's story was simple. He had been brought to the hospital to die. A few days before my visit, he had returned in his heart to his Southern Baptist upbringing, and his childhood home where he'd been surrounded by love. Ken had been brought up by the principles of the Bible. Early in his life, he had accepted Jesus.

As a young man in Atlanta, however, Ken experimented with the homosexual life-style. Eventually he contracted AIDS. Ken was intelligent, and he was acquainted with the facts. As his physical strength waned, his mind and heart returned to his childhood values. He confessed his sins to God and returned to Him. He also turned back to his family, freely expressed love to his mother and sister, and shared with them about the changes Jesus had wrought in his life.

"I learned that my sister had prayed for me for years," he told me, "and my mother had never given up. Now, because of their prayers I'm safe. I have renounced homosexuality. Whether I live or die, I am clean before God!"

His testimony electrified me. *How desperately I need to feel that same thing,* I thought. *There is no question of my salvation, but how I'd love to be where Ken is spiritually at this moment!*

"Some former associates visited me here," he related. "I told them how Jesus had freed me from homosexuality. They resisted every word. They said that I'm experiencing denial, that it's part of the disease, and that Christianity is just a myth that isn't valid for intelligent people." He rested a moment.

"I pray for them," he finished.

Clean before God. That's the essence of the gospel, and Ken had caught it perfectly. If he could experience that cleansing and feel forgiven, couldn't I believe God for grace to that degree? Yes, I could.

When we prayed for God to heal Ken Simmons, I knew in my heart that the answer had arrived long before our prayer—Ken's healing was complete.

I was right. Within days, Ken was transformed from

this life and entered the one for which he had been so gloriously prepared. He went gladly, full of gratitude to God.

Clean before God. That testimony was Ken Simmons's legacy to me—a promise as radiant as the glory that shone from a young man's face and flooded a small, drab room where he lay dying.

To experience the blessing of total self-forgiveness, of course, we must make it our first intention to forgive freely. In my case, I had many such opportunities to forgive! At that time I received bundles of letters from pastors, lay Christians, and other people who plainly didn't like Anita Bryant. Letter after letter contained various degrees of scolding, chastisement, or expressions of disappointment. Eventually, I reasoned that people wouldn't write such letters unless they cared for me, but even today those judgmental expressions still hurt.

There were many individual Christian ministers (some who had utilized my services at their crusades or from their pulpits in the past) who now saw fit to denounce me. Just as I began to make tiny steps toward healing, it seemed another such episode would occur.

Slowly, doggedly, I learned to ask God's forgiveness for the anger and rage I felt after being condemned by too "pious Christians." I'm a stubborn woman, and often it was hard to pray for those who persecuted me. "Lord, I forgive the homosexuals who attacked me," I sometimes told Him. "I understand that. But why is it so hard for me to forgive certain Christian pastors who judge me without knowing any of the facts or intents of hearts."

It can become easier. Once we decide to forgive, God supplies the grace. We learn to shrug off the hurts. We learn not to internalize the attacks, but to pray for our attackers.

I believe that when we obey God's commandment to

pray for those who spitefully use us, something super-natural happens. Not only do we forgive, but we forget the words we once felt sure would scar us for life.

One morning while living in Atlanta I answered the doorbell of my townhouse. Standing there was a well-known minister I hadn't seen for years. His purpose was transparent and straightforward. He had come to Atlanta on other business, but God had told him to seek me out and ask my forgiveness. I felt flabbergasted, uncomfortable, and amazed.

"What do you mean?" I asked.

"I judged you. I said uncharitable things about you. God has convicted me of how I treated you several years ago, and I need your forgiveness."

The tears that mingled with our prayers represented, for me, grateful recognition that God somehow had drawn me close to the concept that forgiveness is a *necessity*. Had I not forgiven this brother, our reconciliation might have been stormy and painful, or it might never have happened. Instead, we experienced love, peace, and joy.

For a year or two, that scene was reenacted every several weeks. To my amazement, some of America's greatest men of God humbled themselves to ask *me* to forgive *them*.

This taught me some unforgettable lessons about the believer's life in Christ. It also convinced me once again—though I never did doubt it—that God has raised up some righteous leaders in America, and that He has blessed our land through these men. Years later (1990) while attending a Presidential Prayer Breakfast I timidly walked over to Billy Graham, and he shocked me by giving me an overwhelming bear hug. He exclaimed how he and Ruth had prayed many times for me and my family during those darkest hours but didn't know how to reach me.

God also raised up an army of lay Christian men and women who wrote, wired, and telephoned for years to convey their love, support, and prayers. Had I not been led of God, through Bobbie Ames, to renounce my human resentments and attempt to begin to forgive, as Christ Himself forgives me, do you suppose I could have opened my heart to receive those waves of love? I think not.

When we stand in the wreckage of our own sin, failure, or tragedy, God stands with us. Our efforts at forgiveness and reconciliation draw us closer to Him. In turn, the Lord draws others closer to us, to minister to us.

I didn't want to forgive. I thought my anger was so enormous I never could forgive. The important thing is: no matter what you're feeling, give your will to be willing. Today I view forgiveness as the first plank in the platform of total healing.

"I was in Bible College, going through rough times," my second cousin Kirby King wrote. "I knew you were going through rough times also, and I wanted to encourage you. I was at the point of giving up. I couldn't help anyone the way I felt.

"I asked you how you were able to handle all the persecution, and you said something to me that I never forgot. You said, 'I can do all things through Christ, who strengthens me.' I was only two months old in the Lord. I saw joy on your face and the faith to go on. I made up my mind that no matter what I thought of myself, no matter what man said about me or could do to me, I was going all the way for Christ. Nothing was going to stop me from fulfilling my calling in Christ.

"I rededicated my life to Jesus and walked away that night a new man. The first 'open door' that came to me was missions to England, and I've been there ever since." Signed "Your missionary to England," the letter reminds me of what I so easily might have forfeited—the forgiveness that frees us from self and gives Jesus access to our inner person.

Kirby's letter vividly reminded me that forgiveness is an

endless chain with countless links. God holds each of us responsible for our separate links of the chain. Should we fail, the chain breaks—thus thwarting God's influence, which flows from my link to others along the chain.

Don't ever think it's the easy road, but obedience is the key, regardless of our feelings. Unforgiveness towards anyone would have harmed my prayer efforts for Kirby King, my missionary to England.

Having experienced much criticism, ridicule, and hatred, I suppose I'll always feel compassion for others in that situation, regardless of whether they seem to deserve such fallout. The fact is, I've received in full measure the compassion and forgiveness of my Lord Jesus Christ. How can I offer my hurting brother or sister anything less?

When evangelist Jim Bakker fell into disgrace, I felt moved to write him a letter from my heart. I sensed all too well the sort of communications he must have been receiving, and besides I was painfully aware of how quickly people forget the good done by a public figure who makes a mistake. I remembered that the only major media available to me during my stand in Dade County were Jim Bakker's "PTL" show and Pat Robertson's "700 Club." I was able to share the real truth that this was an unconstitutional bad law that would apply only to private religious schools. It would allow those homosexuals who were proud of their sin, with no desire to change themselves but to change the laws, to flaunt before our children in Christian schools a life-style that is totally against the Scriptures. From the depths of my own recent experiences, I wrote Jim Bakker.

"I hate with a passion what you're doing to yourself and everyone around you, but I'm writing to say I love you in the Lord; and more importantly, God, the Creator of this universe and the Creator of your body, soul, and spirit, loves you just as you are!

"He longs to deliver you from your personal hell, to forgive all your past sins. There is nothing that isn't forgivable with the blood of Jesus Christ. Satan is the accuser and reminder of our past sins and shortcomings. He is quite capable of condemning us to stay in our own personal hell, but only if we give him that authority!

"By faith in Jesus Christ we can tell the devil to flee and by faith put ourselves on the cross [meaning identification with His death], repent, and claim our total forgiveness. God not only wipes the slate clean, but removes it as far as the east is from the west. The blood of Jesus is sufficient, holy, and powerful enough to cover the past, present, and future sins of the whole world.

"How can we be so boastful as to think we have something in our lives that He can't forgive or an addiction that He can't cure? Oh, we of little faith!

"Come up higher, Jim. Jesus is asking you not to hold back anything, but to give yourself lock, stock, and barrel to Him! 'Faithful is he that calleth you, who also will do it' (1 Thess. 5:24). I should know—He did it for me, and He's no respector of persons."

The apostle Paul exhorts us to "comfort one another with the comfort wherewith ye have been comforted." I could write those words to my hurting brother only because my friend Bobbie Ames first led me to trust God with my own baby steps toward obedience, despite the emotions pulling me in the opposite direction. When I willed myself to begin to forgive—*and only then*—could I receive God's overwhelming *forgiveness of me*.

I was sure forgiving was right. I was also certain it seemed impossible to do. But what I didn't consider was that in the event of future marriage—impossible as that was to imagine—forgiveness would be essential.

God can't build any good relationship or marriage on a foundation of hatred, anger, and mistrust.

2

Lord, Help Me Handle My Fears

*F*or the first time, I understood those who commit suicide. I felt I'd never take my own life, but I came close a couple of times, and I understood why others might. I lived with fear. I understood raw despair.

I remember the woman who said, "Lean not on the arm of flesh, Anita." A woman with a husband. A woman who didn't have to earn a living. What did she know about fear? As I learned, maybe you can't define fear, but you surely know it when you feel it. You know it in the middle of the night, when you wake up for no reason and stare into blackness, aware of your trembling body, cold beneath the blankets. Yes, you recognize sheer terror. Maybe it's even worse if you've never lived through those feelings before.

My Grandpa Berry, who was blinded in a terrible Oklahoma oil-refinery accident, was my first hero. Grandpa was there when I learned to walk and talk. He discovered the big voice in this toddler he took care of and encouraged her to sing. He'd make a sound, and I'd respond in one of my big, booming baby wails, and it would tickle him to pieces. He'd say, "Sing, Anita," and I'd "sing," and he'd let out this huge, wonderful laugh.

When I was two, Grandpa talked the preacher into letting me sing "Jesus Loves Me" before the whole church. I did it—I'd do anything for Grandma and Grandpa

Berry—and got smothered in the love, hugs, and applause of the congregation. I loved getting all that attention.

The point is that Grandpa Berry programmed me. He taught me from babyhood that I could do anything I needed to do. I adored my grandpa, and if he said something I didn't think twice. "You can do it," he'd encourage me, and off I'd go. Early on, Grandpa Berry dubbed me the "brave one." I believed him.

The brave one did all sorts of childhood daredevil stunts and got away with most of them. The brave one also learned to tackle assignments most other kids wouldn't dream of doing—singing before *adults,* for goodness' sake; dressing up and going out on stage at civic clubs, county fairs, and PTA meetings. At eight, I sang on radio each week. At twelve, I had my first television show and a voice coach.

Those things were good. I wanted them. No adult pushed me or made me do any of it. My ambitions made me strive toward adult-sized goals, and each attainment boosted my self-confidence a little higher. Brave? Grandpa Berry said I was, so I must be. And if any situation seemed bigger than usual, newer, or stranger—if I got butterflies in my tummy, even to the point of throwing up—I learned I could handle it. Just hang in there, practice, try hard, work until you master it. And, above all, don't let fear stop you.

Grandpa Berry was behind me all the way. Because of him, I honestly believe I missed most of the usual childhood fears. I can still hear his encouraging words, so full of faith in me: "You can do it, Anita!"

Then came reality. Reality is divorce. Reality means losing your home and job and, for some, even losing your children. If all this isn't enough, you wonder how you'll take care of your kids. How can you feed and clothe them? Where will you live? What if, while unintentionally smashing your own life to pieces, you also have ruined their lives? These fears are real, important, and immediate. They engender big-time stress.

My stress symptoms became physical. At times I experienced chest pains for long periods of time or had trouble breathing. Sometimes I choked on my food. Always, I felt overwhelming anxiety, isolation, and a dull, continuous exhaustion.

Later I learned that package of symptoms represents a textbook case of extreme fear. At the time, I actually condemned myself for those fears (good Christians aren't supposed to be fearful, are they?), which of course helped to perpetuate the cycle.

What are the facts about fear? As I said, I was too embarrassed to ask. I was into denial. First, of course, everyone has fears. Fear is a God-given survival mechanism, a warning signal like the fever that signals infection. Our fears represent our intelligence at work, but it's how we process "fear information" that counts!

Through knowing many other men and women who've endured crisis and struggle, you learn that your most horrible fears aren't unique. For example, I know individuals who admit they're afraid to open their mailboxes because they can't face the contents. Thousands of people these days feel terrified—justifiably—of being accosted by their former spouses. And others allow telephones to ring and ring because they're afraid to answer. The fear list seems endless.

The more intense your personality, the closer to the surface your feelings, the more you're likely to experience a wide variety of fears, with a wild catalog of manifestations. I should have realized that my own terrors fit right in with my highly emotional personality.

As fear immobilizes us, we perceive a number of physical distress signals: sweating; rapid heartbeat; weakness in knees and legs; tightness in the chest; hyperventilation; shortness of breath; inability to swallow; dry mouth;

sometimes even blurred vision, dizziness, or the shakes. As such symptoms escalate into overwhelming fear, our physiological reactions are signaling an all-out panic attack. We need help. Our normal fear signals have gone haywire.

How does a fear-ridden person climb out of such a morass? Certainly I believed I never could. My divorce had followed an unbelievable year of national notoriety, work, public statements, policy meetings, and press appearances—in addition to my full-time duties as wife and mother and a career that was going full-tilt. No wonder I had to push any fears that emerged into the background!

Even when network reporters phoned our house to "verify" reports of my death, or bomb squad members with trained dogs searched our home for explosives, or we received threats against the children—even at such times, God protected my family and me with an invisible shield nothing seemed to penetrate. My life was threatened constantly, but because I truly was not afraid, but full of faith, my children worked through their fears and became strong in the Lord. God carried my children through months of indescribably abnormal stresses, and they emerged with no severe personality damage. He kept each of us from the ravages of fear.

How then could I walk from that encircling protection, which I knew in moment-to-moment certainty, into a later situation of darkness and pure torment? Easily. The warfare against me was so ferocious and vicious that it wore me down and when attacks came from some of those closest to me, the hurt was more than I could bear. Satan deceived me, I took my eyes off the Lord and put them within myself and on my deteriorating circumstances. I became convinced that I'd forfeited God's protection. This thought, incidentally, did not come from God!

I write about this now became it's so important to realize how Satan attacks our minds and tries to subvert everything we know about the gospel. For example, a very close Christian sister told me that because of my divorce, God's curse would follow me throughout my life and throughout the lives of my children and grandchildren. Think about that statement for even a moment, and you realize it ignores everything the believer has known about God's mercy, forgiveness, and grace. Still, the words haunted me. I hated divorce then and I still do, but there are times when a relationship is far more destructive for everyone to stay in than to get out. Yes, the ramifications are terrible for all concerned, but sometimes there's no other way to survive and have peace.

Then came the time at Mama's house in Oklahoma, where the children and I had retreated (June of 1980, where we would sojourn for eleven months), when I received a copy of a telegram an evangelist sent to the governor of Oklahoma. Our governor had called for a day of prayer because the state was suffering a protracted drought. This Christian brother informed him that our nation suffers such disasters as drought because of sinners like Anita Bryant!

I began to read that message but couldn't finish it. I handed it to Mama and began to cry, then went to bed and lay in a fetal position for three days during which I couldn't stop crying. I thought, *My life is over. Why can't I die?*

I had no strength to pray. I lay there and hurt all over, unable to eat or sleep. Waves of guilt, fear, pain, and rejection alternated with the wish for death. I couldn't think, not even about God. It was total, dark isolation, as if I were in hell. I believed that never again would there be a life for me.

If that agonizing episode represented the lowest period of my life, it also gave birth to the most shining truth I cherish. During those three days of inexpressible suffering, I felt the Lord with me. Though anguished, somehow I knew I was in the arms of God, who held me like a loving parent would cradle their little baby. I knew He was there and that He loved me unconditionally.

Never can I imagine or begin to describe anything more terrifying than those three days. But, never will I forget that at life's lowest point when there seems no end to your weakness, when it seems you'll fall and fall forever, underneath are the everlasting arms of our loving Heavenly Father. He will not let us fall.

We can be overcomers. There are ways to conquer paralyzing fears, and we can learn them. I soon discovered that the first step was telling the truth. As Grandpa Berry's brave one, I didn't like admitting to terror. Fear went against my self-image. But months of physical stress, fatigue, and abnormal circumstances had taken their toll, and I couldn't hide my fears from anyone.

That was good. Denial really doesn't help at all. It simply delays healing. What we need to do is acknowledge our fears and begin to face them. There's no need to feel shame, of course, since fear represents normal warning signals—not something that deserves self-punishment. The Bible doesn't admonish us about feeling fear, but about choosing to live according to its tyranny.

As we learn, often the hard way, running away solves nothing. Only by confronting our fears can we overcome them. Somewhere during that time I heard a teaching on Ephesians 6:11-18, in which the apostle Paul calls on us to "put on the whole armor of God" (v.11). He speaks in the language of first-century warfare, listing the separate parts of that armor: sword, shield, breastplate, shoes, and so on. However, in light of recent wars, we can better understand the purposes of armor. This powerful Scripture always had been a favorite passage, but that day I learned something I never knew before: in New Testament times there was no armor to protect one's back.

Only by *facing* our enemies can we prevail. Face your fears, and with God's help, those very fears become the catalyst for an overcoming faith.

Later I was to notice how many times the psalmist David talks to God about fear. *He should know,* I thought, *considering the life he led—hunted like an animal; hiding behind rocks or within caves; running from armies; fleeing the insane King Saul, who ordered David's death*.

How did David handle that harrowing life-style? In Psalms 56:3 he says, "What time I am afraid, I will trust in thee." He went to the Source of courage and protection. No wonder believers recite the Psalms when they need courage! Psalm 37 also became a favorite of mine during this time.

Returning to work represented a major challenge in my dealings with fear. I dreaded work. I had no desire to sing, no heart or head for business, and I loathed the thought of any mention in the press. Work obstacles—time pressures, meeting the press and public, always having to live in a glass fishbowl—literally made me weep with frustration and fear, but I had no choice. My head told me I needed to return to normal life. My gut told me I couldn't.

Fortunately, I listened to my head. I could not have done it without the encouragement and help of my dear friend, James Lyon of Houston, Texas, who not only believed in me and my talent, but had the courage and the commitment to make it happen. He brought together a group of business advisors and friends and began the necessary steps to rebuild my career. A brilliant young man named Seth Marshall was hired as my manager. It was his job to tiptoe through the long list of "Sorry, noes" and "too controversials." Seth was smart enough not to let me see the long list of turndowns. He was afraid it would make me crumble, and he was right.

Eventually, though, he came in waving a contract. His big smile advertised the coup of the century—a weeklong engagement! Immediately I burst Seth's bubble. He had landed a supper-club job, and I told Seth I didn't do supper clubs.

We nearly had a pitched battle. Seth pointed out that the price was right, that the engagement was a solid one in a well-known club with impeccable credentials. Starting in Canada was a plus, Seth argued, an excellent place to try out the new act and boost my self-confidence. Plus, Seth's friend David Benoit, a superb jazz musician, would be my pianist-conductor.

I felt playing the Top Hat Supper Club in Windsor, Ontario, turned out to be a divine appointment, but you couldn't have convinced me that opening night. Fifteen people showed up!

Terror and despair rolled over me like a Canadian cold wave. What now? I'd prayed, practiced, rehearsed, worked—and now this. In all my career, I'd never faced such humiliation.

Mike Drakitch, the Top Hat's owner and manager, politely wondered about the tiny turnout. Mike had operated thirty years featuring such luminaries as Rich Little, Giselle MacKenzie, Rick Nelson, and Teresa Brewer.—and now this. He was used to packed houses. So was I.

My worst horrors had materialized. "Ask Mike to see me, please," I said to Seth. "Maybe he'd like to cancel our contract." When Seth started to object, I withered him with a look. The next day, I took a deep breath and leveled with Mike. I told him about the homosexuals' boycott against me in the U.S. and how their fear tactics had cost me eighty bookings in one year. Mike looked incredulous, but I plunged ahead to tell him I honestly didn't know whether I could still draw an audience. There—the truth was out. Mike looked very stern, so I drew a deep breath and asked, "Do you want to cancel my contract?"

Mike's reaction was immediate. "Never," he roared, placing his big hand over mine for emphasis. "We'll go ahead as planned. If they don't come, you perform anyhow. You have a great show!"

"But you're losing money."

"I don't care," he insisted stubbornly. "That's not important. It is important that you don't quit." Then he told me his story.

Mike Drakitch was a young man at the end of World War II, when his native Yugoslavia came under Soviet dominance. He remembered seeing trains pass through his hometown, taking countless young men like himself somewhere. "Where, I didn't ever know," he said, shrugging, "but my brothers and I knew our turn would come. One by one, we boys left our country. We traveled on foot."

Telling no one of their plans, each Drakitch brother made his escape. Nick, Mike's older brother, reached Canada, worked hard, and bought a restaurant. One night Mike, like his brothers, left home. He began a pattern of walking from point to point, always at night, for hundreds of dangerous miles in the darkness. Weeks later, he crossed the border into Italy and freedom.

Mike worked in Italy for several months until he could afford to join Nick in Canada. He started his new life as a dishwasher in his brother's restaurant. Years of hard work and determined saving enabled him eventually to buy a rundown, bankrupt restaurant, which he restored and operated with ever-increasing success—the Top Hat.

Mike told me that because of his own hardships he understood, far more than most, how important it is for an individual never to bow to coercion. The sixteen-hour days he worked to build the Top Hat represented, in his mind, marvelous years of freedom and opportunity. He understood the dignity of work. He knew that we must stand up to personal fear. Everything he told me put iron in my soul.

This engagement had a happy postscript. Detroit newspapers just across the border carried good feature stories and praised the act. Americans, as well as Canadians, crowded into the restaurant.

Each evening waiters delivered notes written on napkins, business cards, or anything else: "We're proud of you, Anita." "Don't ever quit." "We're praying for you." "We love you." If you wrote one of those notes, I probably still have it. I took each of them as a message from the Lord. Never has His encouragement to me been received with more gratitude!

God honored Mike Drakitch's stand, and The Top Hat prospered that week. So did I. I had faced some of my worst fears and conquered them. As for Mike Drakitch, I felt that he, his lovely wife Mary, and their four fine sons had served as agents of the Lord. Their faith, courage, and refusal to submit to fear galvanized me into action. Because Mike stood with me then, I perform today not with fear, but with joy.

I won't pretend that fear never returned. But I began to learn ways to defeat the spirit of fear and live my life. For example . . .

Take action. I began to isolate those things that terrified me and decided what action to take. Even if all I could manage was a baby step, I learned it was important to follow through on my decisions.

Don't try to do it alone. I recall soon after my move to Atlanta in 1984 that the Atlanta Press Club asked me to appear as the "mystery guest" at their Christmas party. Nothing felt scarier than facing a roomful of journalists and their antagonistic questions.

I knew I'd have to meet the "enemy" sometime, of course, so why not all of them at once? I asked two friends to accompany me, took a deep breath, and waded into no-man's-land. It didn't take long for a talk-show host to corner me and needle me about views obviously at the opposite pole from my own. "Tell me how you feel about abortion," he asked, waving an obvious red flag in my face.

"I don't think you want to talk with me about abortion, because I have a very biased viewpoint," I replied. That disconcerted him, but he persisted.

"I have a brilliant, handsome, very gifted son, and he's adopted," I told the reporter. "I simply can't be objective about that subject. I do believe that women should control their own bodies, though, but the control needs to be applied *before* they get pregnant, not after the fact. Once pregnant, a woman is dealing not only with her body but also with a child's life and a father's offspring. It isn't too difficult to control one's body by abstaining from sex but, if one chooses not to abstain, then one should be prepared for the responsibility of having a child."

At once the man's challenging demeanor changed. No longer did he attempt to outwit me conversationally but instead turned into a charming, interested, *human* individual. We got along fine from that moment on.

Because my two friends encouraged me to do the thing I feared, I could attend a wonderful party, sing to the journalists, and have a ball!

Dress up to tackle the lions. If you stay home, stop dressing like a scrub lady. If you work outside the home, outfit yourself as well as possible and try to look as though you can handle anything. I know a woman who wears a red slip under her gray or navy-blue outfit whenever she has to do anything she hates. If red gives you courage, wear it!

Step up your pace. Defeated people always seem to slump and shuffle. The antidote is to move faster and work faster. I tried to add simple new routines to my daily list: volunteering for a job at the kids' school, helping with a community fund-raiser, even planting some tomatoes in the backyard. This helps. When your tomatoes succeed, you succeed. Little accomplishments empower us and help drive away fear.

Smile more. I didn't want to smile. Sometimes I was so afraid, my face felt paralyzed. That couple looking at me—do they hate me? Will they say something spiteful in front of other people? I learned that smiling fights off paranoia. Even a fake smile relaxes you, and a good, broad smile advertises self-confidence. Proverbs 15:13a says, "A merry heart maketh a cheerful countenance."

Smile when you are scared. You need it. More importantly, your kids need it!

Help others. Sometimes I had to force myself to cook something for a needy family, or even to be willing to pray with someone who needed prayer. But I soon learned that focusing on other people made me forget whatever terrors might be assaulting me at the moment. Anything we do for others helps liberate us from our own problems and fears.

Be good to yourself. Demoralizing fear is the worst disease I know, and for a long time I was afraid I might be crippled by it. Friends helped me not to despise myself. I learned it was OK to give myself small treats and the extra care that serves to banish illness. Exercise helps. Music helps. Beauty helps. Give yourself these things.

Realize that this, too, shall pass. At one time I didn't believe it, but all nightmares eventually end. Even when I thought my life had come to a screeching, irreversible halt, for some reason I began to use, unconsciously, King David's formula: "What time I am afraid, I will trust in thee" (Ps. 56:3).

Fear intrudes on every life. We're built to overcome all fears.

3
Meeting That Strange Woman—Myself!

"Everything seems to depend on me, and I feel paralyzed. I can't make decisions. I don't know what I want, and I'm out of work with no way to make a living. I can't get a handle on anything, because my identity has slipped.

"Life feels empty, semiautomatic, mechanical. I have stopped doing the things that are normal to do. I don't socialize. I see only my family.

"Actually, I long to come to a complete stop, just remain in the fetal position."

I wrote those words ten years ago. Judging from my mail, they might have been written by thousands of other people. They are the thoughts of persons *in extremis,* in crisis far beyond anything they have imagined or experienced.

Extreme crisis—in my case, the crisis of divorce—forced me to meet and deal with a woman I had neglected for years: *myself.* My mind flicks back to a scene in the grocery store soon after my world collapsed. I was trying to buy food for four instead of six, and suddenly I found myself hanging onto the cart and violently shaking and weeping. *I couldn't do it.* I had to flee from the store because I thought I would disintegrate—stomp up and down, scream, or do something terrible right there.

Several other woman have told me about similar grocery-store incidents, except they were trying to shop for one—themselves—and found they had no idea of what they needed or liked. "I had absolutely no preferences," one woman said. "For years I 'wanted' whatever everybody else wanted. Now I had to choose for myself, and could not imagine what I really liked to eat."

The Chinese character for _crisis_ embodies two meanings: _danger_ and _opportunity_. The newly divorced feel extremely threatened, standing by the grocery cart with no inkling of who we are or what we want. At that moment you don't see opportunity. You don't know yourself in your new role as an _individual_.

I quickly learned that in many ways I did not know myself at all. Role playing was second nature to me, onstage and off. I had been trained to do it well, for the show must always go on. To me, my entertainer's role always ranked far below others—wife, mother, Christian, churchwoman, friend—yet it represented an always visible, high-profile self. I never could escape the Anita Bryant singer person, not even in the grocery store. That part of me always had to look perfectly fresh, perfectly happy, and perfectly well-dressed. Above all, she couldn't be seen crying in the grocery store!

The role I did neglect was the most fundamental of all—that of woman, person, human being, _me_. I knew that Jesus instructs us to "love thy neighbor as thyself," but I had no idea of how to love myself. Not only did I not realize that I did not relate to myself well, that I did not like myself in some ways or even have a healthy self-concept, but I could not see how much that lack of self-esteem had also robbed my other relationships.

A Texas woman described the syndrome in a letter to me: "I have been single for eleven years, and it has been difficult to find my place. I am mother, father, cook, breadwinner, etc. I know that without God I could not have made it to this day.

"I think the hardest struggle is with personal identity. I

don't like to identify myself as a divorcee. It bears the impression of being a failure, reject, whatever else the devil can find to throw in.

"Thus I find it is my identity I am ashamed of."

Because she is fighting the good fight as God is on her side, I feel confident this woman will find the answers she needs. God is so faithful. But her letter well delineates the struggle to know oneself. Her needs echo those of thousands of other individuals today. Bookstore shelves overflowing with "pop" psychology books purporting to solve the "identity problem" prove my point.

If you have never learned to love yourself as well as others, you probably learned to repress your true feelings and look elsewhere for self-esteem: work, marriage, children, property, or position. Many people define their identities by such roles or symbols.

When crisis comes, however, those compensations fail us. That's when you feel terrible personal inadequacies: mistrust of others and yourself, weakness, shame, fear of looking within. One self-help group, Codependents Anonymous, lists these signs of impaired emotions:

I assume responsibility for others' feelings and behaviors.

I have difficulty identifying or expressing feelings.

I have difficulty in forming and maintaining close relationships.

I have difficulty making decisions.

I am afraid of being hurt or rejected by others.

I tend to put other people's wants and needs first.

My self-esteem is bolstered by outer influences. I cannot acknowledge good things about myself.

I tend to minimize, alter, or even deny the truth about how I feel.

I do not know that being vulnerable and asking for help are OK and normal.

People who join Codependents Anonymous admit that they are powerless over others and that their lives have become unmanageable. Then they acknowledge that "a power greater than ourselves could restore us to sanity." Thank God, I knew that Power, that Person—Jesus Christ, the Son of the living God.

Emotionally needy Christians, and there are many of us beneath the masks we wear, possess a rock-firm platform on which the "identity question" stands: *I am made in God's image*.

The search for self begins exactly here, before the throne of God. God made me. He knew me before the foundation of the world. God has a plan for my life. The prophet Jeremiah wrote (Jer. 29:11, NASB), "'For I know the plans that I have for you,' declares the Lord, 'plans for welfare and not for calamity to give you a future and a hope.'"

Charles Colson wrote: "For a generation, western society has been obsessed with the search for self. We've tried to bring meaning into life through Yoga, awareness workshops, creative consciousness, est, TA—each fad with an avid following until something new comes along.

"The not-so-magnificent obsession to 'find ourselves' has spawned a whole set of counterfeit values: we worship fame, success, materialism, and celebrity. It is an insidious disease called 'me-ism.'"

The antidote? At the risk of sounding simplistic, our only answer is in knowing God through Christ Jesus our Lord, for only in knowing Him can we possibly know ourselves. Further, it is only through loving and trusting Him that we learn to love and trust ourselves.

Of course, the heartbroken woman pushing the grocery cart that day didn't dream that her desperate *poverty of spirit* was to be fed with Christ's own provision, a fundamental personality healing. Though I often despised myself, I always loved God. Because He loves you and me, He can and will teach us to receive His love, healing, and *joy*.

But why must we *first* know God? If I do not really know myself, who I "see" every day, how can I possibly

know a God I cannot see? Even the greatest saints, someone told me, can encounter that "dark night of the soul"
when they wonder if they ever knew God at all. Did they
delude themselves? Was their faith misplaced? Did they
even have faith?

That's when God and we go back to the basics. In our
struggles we come to understand that we must seek God,
because:

Knowing God makes me desire to be like Him.
Knowing God reveals the truth about myself.
Knowing God enables me to be secure.
Knowing God provides me with abundant life.
Knowing God introduces me to eternity.

If God, not myself, is the primary Person I seek to
know, how may I find Him?

Each of us enters into relationship with God through
three simple means:

1. *By faith.*—Not even great faith, necessarily. Just
enough faith to believe that He is, and to turn to Him.
Find a church of your choice, for "faith cometh by hearing, and hearing by the word of God" (Rom. 10:17), but
make sure they preach the Word of God, not man-made
traditions. Some years ago Tiffany's, the New York jew-
elry firm, sold a pin whose design was formed from two
words: *Try God*. Thousands of people bought and wore
the distinctive lapel ornament, with its never-failing formula. You have to decide to try God.

2. *By prayer.*—The Bible describes God as a "rewarder
of them that diligently seek him" (Heb. 11:6). Jesus told
us to "seek and ye shall find" (Matt. 11:7; Luke 11:9). The
simplest prayer brings us straight into the presence of
God. Anyone who decides to seek God can pray and will
find the One he seeks.

3. *Through reading the Holy Bible.*—I have read the

Bible through several times now, and each time my faith is strengthened, and His light shines in areas that before were dark to me. The books contained in the Bible were written by various men over a 1,600-year time span, as inspired by God the Holy Spirit. They contain more than seven thousand promises the Heavenly Father has given to mankind, and every principle and truth by which we are to live. I like what some people call the Bible—God's love letter to *us*. Open the Bible, and you will find a specific word for your life this moment. It never fails.

By those three simple means, God provides access to Him at all times and in all places. You can enter a new relationship to God at this moment through His Son Jesus Christ. It doesn't matter if you never approached Him before, or if you once knew Him but have turned away. Even if you're not quite convinced in your heart that God exists and that He cares for you, He still wants to hear from you.

You might want to stop right here and take the most important step of your life. *Try God.*

Expect the relationship between God and you to be something totally unique. It's person-to-Person, and it may sometimes be stormy, but always interesting. And when we find ourselves flat on our faces, trying to look up, that's when the strongest bonds become established. Our crisis becomes His opportunity.

During those wretched days when I hated who I was and what my life had become, I learned that the Lord enjoys having divine jokes with me—especially when I tend to become overdramatic. I guess He likes to poke His children in the ribs sometimes, or maybe just likes to hear us laugh.

Then again, my Heavenly Father obviously knows my insecurities and responds to them with such tenderness. I remember when my daughter Gloria was planning her wedding, and I shopped for the perfect mother-of-the-bride dress. I found *the* dress, but it was way out of my price range. Privately I told God how unhappy that made me and how depressed I felt that I could no longer afford to buy exactly the dress I wanted. I told Him I hated to cut corners for my precious daughter's wedding.

That wasn't a "spiritual" prayer, and I don't pretend it was, but it was honest. I turned the dress problem over to Him and virtually forgot about it until almost the last moment. One day, while helping Gloria shop for her trousseau at another store, I discovered a different version of the dress I longed for—same fabric, same color, same manufacturer, but a different style. I liked the second dress much better than the one I thought I wanted, and it was marked down to half price!

Maybe that doesn't sound earthshakingly important to you, but it held tremendous significance to me. I had begun by now to realize how often the Lord's tender, personal presence comes shining through our daily lives. _In the old days, when price tags didn't have to matter so much, could God have spoken to me so specifically? Had I relied on myself and my good life so much that I overlooked His goodness to me? Did I really understand that He cares about every detail of our lives?_

Holding the cloud of pearl-beige silk and lace in my arms and thinking these thoughts, I cried. So did my tenderhearted Gloria, who understood perfectly. Her father paid for most of the wedding, but I had agreed to help Gloria purchase her dress, and my funds were skimpy— but through prayer the Lord had supernaturally provided a way for us to purchase her perfect wedding dress. She knew my dress meant very little, but His love means everything. It felt overwhelming.

Take away the husband or wife, the job, the community, the bank account, the life-style, and you are left with one man or woman and our God. When everything is stripped from us and we, like babes, feel totally naked before Him, He calls us by name—"Anita Jane, My daughter"—and allows us to feel our sonship or daughtership as we never comprehended it before.

Out of the chaos we make of our lives, the Lord waits, ready and able to build a whole, healthy, and holy new person. Our "image" has been shattered, but He replaces that with something far better—our personhood. His "new creation" is someone we can like and enjoy.

The old "life-style" we built and cherished—and grieved over losing—had to go. It no longer fits. The new person stops looking back, takes his or her eyes off circumstances, and begins to look ahead. Instead of a stale "life-style," we choose abundant life.

4

My Family—My Fortress

"God [sets] the solitary in families," the Bible says (Ps. 68:6).

After my painful divorce in 1980, my heart led me home to my family, straight as a homing pigeon—back to the rugged Oklahoma oil country where I grew up. Most of them were still there, just as I remembered them—my mother and her husband "Paw Paw" George Cate, my father Warren, whom everyone calls "Blackie, with his wife Jewel, my half-brother Sonny, two stepsisters, and their families, plus a huge tribe of uncles, aunts, cousins, and kissin' kin . . . and close by in Texas, my sister Sandra Page, her husband Sam and their three daughters and husbands, Kathy and Joey Odom, Lisa and Randy Willard, and Michelle and Pat Eitel.

Lenora Cate, my mother, is the kind of friend you need when bad things happen. Independent and feisty as I've been all my life, I admit I still want my mama when trouble strikes. She is like a rock. Daddy George, my stepfather, is the same. He didn't say one word when I piled in—bringing teenage Bobby and Gloria, plus twins Billy and Barbara, who were twelve—for an indefinite stay.

It was the most miserable period of my life, and my family acutely sensed it. I could not and did not function. Others took care of my children while I attempted— mostly unsuccessfully—to sort out my life.

It still embarrasses me to recall what it must have cost my parents. Tending to four children is one thing—a daughter with total nervous exhaustion is another. Meanwhile, adding to the chaos, newsmen camped outside the house, and photographers continually drove up, hoping to shoot yet another picture of their exhausted subject. Additionally, as if that weren't enough, the telephone rang and rang—news hounds seeking interviews or asking Mama how she "felt" about my return to Oklahoma.

Words cannot describe my wonderful, ordinary, everyday, close-knit family. They represent middle-class America, traditional values, strength, a gamut of occupations and talents. We have singers, music teachers and artists. We also have several ministers on the Berry family side. The Bryants are mostly ranchers, oilfield and blue-collar workers. All work hard, stand fast, and close ranks when something happens to one of us.

This time it was Anita Jane. I wanted to respond to their love and concern, but couldn't. Those days I could only receive. "Sweet Anita," a cousin would murmur, "We love you so much, darlin'. Don't worry. It'll be all right."

Those reassurances came and came, and it seemed I just couldn't respond—couldn't be myself. I wondered if I ever would be the same Anita they'd always known before. *Surely,* I thought to myself, *I'm too changed. I'll never be Anita Jane Bryant again. She got lost somewhere along the way.*

Then came the first weekend in June and our tremendous family reunion. How I shrank from the thought of braving the whole crowd! I just couldn't. The thought of seeing Aunt Marie and Uncle Luther Berry, for example, made me flinch. Uncle Luther, Mama's older brother, has been one of the most important, and favorite, people in my life. He's also a retired Southern Baptist minister.

I thought I knew Uncle Luther's views on divorce. He probably wouldn't accost me with those views, but even so, I couldn't bear to see the look of sadness and disappointment in his eyes. He thought a lot of me, and I felt I had let him down. I couldn't bear the pain.

This time, Mama stood firm. No, I would not stay home. I would attend the reunion. Everybody expected me, and they wouldn't ask me to sing. Sing! That's the last thing I could have done. But since there was no way out, I went to the reunion with everybody else. Mama's mind was made up.

The day went by in a blur of colors, voices, and laughter. Happy, joking people. Kids drinking too many colas and eating too much chicken. Somebody brought my favorite blackberry cobbler, and I ate a few bites after all. One by one, people came to hug me, say a few words, remind me they'd always loved me, and very gradually, little by little, something happened in my heart. The hurt, terror, and emptiness began to ease.

Then I saw Uncle Luther walking toward me. Against my will, I dropped my eyes. Then he stood before me, his arms wrapped around me, and I felt the familiar warmth of my Uncle Luther's huge hug.

I flinched momentarily. Then my pastor uncle spoke the healing words: "What's the matter, Anita? I just want to love on you a little bit!"

With that the dam burst. Uncle Luther wiped my tears, teased me a little, laughed some, shared a few funny family anecdotes, and everything changed.

Suddenly I saw the brilliant sunlight and smelled the fresh outdoors. I heard barking dogs and giggling children, car doors slamming, the sound of the ice-cream churn. Things felt familiar—right.

I wandered from cousin to cousin, making small talk. I played on the swing, feeling the movement, the fresh air on my face, remembering how it felt when I was a child. I ate somebody's fresh ice cream and somebody else's cake. It was all very ordinary, yet so amazingly extraordinary— those beautiful, caring people who belong to me, those people who were taking care of me and my children without a thought of their own comfort or convenience.

That day I learned to receive. I stood under a big tree,

watching them all, my kinfolks, as they came and went, realizing how unstintingly they gave to me, and receiving their goodness in my spirit. Heaven knows I always loved and appreciated my family, and felt proud of them, but that day I thanked God for each individual in our big tribe.

You see, God has provided a place for each of us. Our families are meant to offer respite, encouragement, and healing. Mine did, and does. But what God showed me was that I had always been too independent. I needed my family, and I needed to realize that.

Sometimes divorce or other kinds of personal failure tend to estrange individuals from their families. What desolation you see on their faces! I think of a mother I knew who, after several years, "forgave" her daughter for divorcing a man who had abused her. The young woman suffered more from the loss of her mother's love than from any of the rest of her anguish.

Think what happens, though, when a family gathers around one who falls. That person, once restored, treasures those relationships more than ever before, and is available to "comfort [others with] the comfort wherewith we ourselves are comforted" (2 Cor. 1:4).

Perhaps you may have few, if any, family members available. Maybe you are talking back to me right now, saying, "Anita, that's just great, for you, but I don't really have a family." Yes, you do. You have the family of God. Find your brothers and sisters through Christ and His church—in a group of Bible-believing Christians who have comfort and love one for another. Many people have testified, "The only place I am loved is with God's people."

I was young when my own parents divorced, and the hurt of losing my father did not heal for more than twenty years. Dad found a new wife, Jewel, with three stepdaughters, Norma, Nancy, and Judy who was later killed in an auto accident, and they had Warren Bryant, Jr.

(Sonny), my father's first and only boy. My younger sister Sandra and I were too little (two and three years old) to understand when my parents first divorced. They remarried when we were five and six, then later divorced when we were eleven and twelve, which wounded us deeply, and the rejection became very personal as if we had caused it to happen somehow!

It took quite a while for Mama to begin dating, and at first we couldn't stand George Richard Cate, but we later learned to love "Daddy George," whom Mother eventually married, and from the beginning he loved us as though we were his own.

But our father was gone. Although we visited Dad and his new family from time to time, we had lost the essence of our relationship with him during our growing-up years. For a long time it was like a wound in my heart that never quite healed, until I was thirty-three years old. During a deeper walk with the Lord, He revealed the hate in my heart I had hidden so craftily and carefully over the years and caused me to confess to God and to my dad all those pent-up emotions, and be able to say, "Dad, I forgive you, and I love you unconditionally, no matter what is your side of the story. I no longer have any hidden unforgiveness." That's when, as a married woman with four children, our father-daughter relationship really began, and God has been faithful to make up for lost time. It does not replace my love for Daddy George, who raised me, but the hole in my heart has healed, and my dad and I have a very special bond these days.

When my personal world fell apart, Dad wanted to help me. By then retired from the two-fisted world of the Oklahoma oil fields, he worked a medium-size ranch in the small town of Sasakwa.

I recall a spring morning when Dad tried to counsel his anxious, weary "kid." He had built himself into an excellent businessman before he retired, and he was trying to help me make sense of my tangled affairs.

Wisely, Dad took me into his garden. He is older now, still tanned and muscular but hindered by emphysema and asthma. His illness is acute. Outdoors, though, Dad can breathe better. The world is still and quiet here, and everything feels brand new.

Dad and I are kneeling beside his raised garden beds, weeding and cultivating the tender new plants. It's fascinating to see the beauty of pale-green lettuce plants emerging from the rich, black loam, the young beans, onions and tomatoes, and other good things I can't identify.

My father seems at home, very familiar with the growth process. Grandpa Bryant was a farmer so Dad came by it naturally. He explains how he built the beds—four feet by sixteen—so he can work them from both sides. The boxes contain humus enriched with barnyard manure, and he patiently instructs me on how to combine leaves, grass clippings, and kitchen scraps to make rich compost.

That day is engraved on my mind. An ordinary day, I suppose, to my father. But I felt like a young girl learning the lore her dad feels is important to teach her. That day and many other days to follow made up for all the other years we didn't get to do those things.

I really saw my father that day. I saw that he is wise, and knows and enjoys things of the earth. I could look at him and see that I am really a big part of him. I could listen to his hearty sense of humor and his charismatic ability to tell a story, like Grandpa Bryant used to do, and understand that we are, in so many ways, very much alike.

Despite his chronic illness, my dad doesn't complain. He can't work hard and earn big money like before, but even from total dependence on an oxygen tank he still finds satisfying ways to work. He showed me by example that you take the garbage of your life and turn it into compost. I thank God for my dad, and for Jewel, who has become my friend, my stepsisters, and Sonny, too.

Because of the Ames's and other friends in Selma, but most of all, the Lord's leading, the children and I moved there in June of 1981. Then came that bleak, traumatic first holiday I spent alone. I sent three of the kids to spend Thanksgiving holidays with their father and their older brother Bobby in Miami.

Unwisely, however, I had made no plans for myself. Never before in my life had I been totally alone on any holiday. Worse, we had just moved from Oklahoma to Selma. I knew John and Bobbie Ames, of course, and several other people by now. I had decided not to interfere with my friends' family holiday and to enjoy doing my own thing.

That morning my agitation built to a crescendo. I felt as though I were suffocating. I paced the floor, nearly hyperventilating with anxiety. I was alone, totally alone.

Always I had harbored a tremendous fear of being alone, but most people would never have guessed it, for the fear was hidden deep in my soul. In fact, once I wrote a poem about it. It is probably a common phobia, but I knew my panic attack was overwhelming. I literally was wringing my hands in frustration. Finally I telephoned an out-of-town friend and blurted out the story. I admitted that my fears were so extreme I wished I had a tranquilizer or a bottle of wine!

My friend's suggestion struck me as crazy: "Do something for someone else." How could I help anyone else when I couldn't even help myself? Well, I couldn't. Everybody else was celebrating Thanksgiving Day. They were with their families. *Everybody else had family.*

My friend didn't seem to have much sympathy to offer. "All over America," she said, "people are alone on Thanksgiving Day. Try to be a blessing to someone else who is alone."

OK, but who? I had no idea. Everyone I could think of would be part of a family gathering. I had been invited by several good friends, but I couldn't interrupt their plans.

What to do? At last I did what I should have done to begin with—asked God for direction.

Then I was standing in my unfamiliar new kitchen, pulling out baking utensils. Some time later I lifted the last Florida citrus cake, my specialty, from the oven. Several tall, handsome cakes stood before me. The whole house smelled of sugary, lemony, buttery goodness. I felt excited.

"Lord, what do I do with those cakes?" I queried as I hastily dressed. What in the world would I do with these big cakes!

God *guided* me to a house I otherwise could not have found, the home of an elderly widow I had met when visiting the First Methodist Church. When she appeared at the door I immediately saw she had been crying. She didn't even try to hide the tears or her amazement.

"I told the Lord I was all by myself on Thanksgiving Day!" she exclaimed, "and up walks Anita Bryant and hands me a cake!" She kept exclaiming over my visit as we shared tea and goodies, and before long we were laughing and hugging. It felt wonderful!

My next stop was to take a cake to the families of John and Bobbie Ames, of course, and another to that of Bob and Gloria Crump. Both groups were operating in high gear, and greeted me with screams, hugs, and "Miss Anita, come sit yourself down at this table!"

I was afraid to make the next two family gatherings I felt God was leading me to, and the fear made me argue with the Lord, as I headed my car to the house where some single members of the local press were meeting for Thanksgiving. Journalists work strange hours and, too often, happen to be loners. The hostess, Millie Vick, worked for the *Selma Times Journal,* and she and her husband, Brother, had asked me several times to join them if I didn't make other plans. Another journalist friend Jean Martin, a recent widow, had written a touching story about me for the *Times Journal.* Because we had talked about our single status, she generously invited me to her house, where she lived with her daughter and mother.

Initially, I had turned down their invitations, and I couldn't believe I was actually going. And then I was loading my plate at the Vick's table, laughing, talking, and getting acquainted with the local press corps. These were people I would usually try to avoid—the press! Actually, they were funny, interesting, and kind. We had a ball.

That evening—snug and content with no wine and no tranquilizer, but several Thanksgiving dinners in my tummy—I reflected on my unusual adventures. My kids had called, and sounded surprised and relieved to learn that I had had so much fun. They were also having fun, and I felt glad.

Slowly, as I marveled at the way the Lord had planned my day, I saw a pattern emerge. God sets the solitary in families. He had set me down in families, except for that darling little widow.

Then I saw it in a flash. She and I *together* became a "family." I had not intruded on the two families I visited which seemed so complete, because families always have room for one more. As for the press corps, that diverse group had formed themselves into a family unit.

"Lord, what if I had not asked You to tell me what to do?" I prayed, amazed.

That day I realized some new facets about God's unlimited creativity. Why, He is creating families from all sorts of circumstances and possibilities—neighborhoods, churches, workplaces. All He needs is volunteers!

It is still hard for me to volunteer. A divorcee's confidence is at a low ebb, and there is a strong tendency to avoid any more rejection. There's still a little reserve in me about stepping forward without a specific invitation. But hopefully never again will I weep alone at home, suffering because I feel left out. The church as a whole, I believe, has been remiss in ministering to singles per se, by separating them and by not encouraging solid, whole Chris-

tian families to bring them into their lives. Although many
singles ministries meet a lot of needs, it's my opinion that
perhaps the reason more singles aren't reached, is because even within Christian Families, many husbands or
wives feel threatened or jealous. I've experienced this
personally many times. Isolation in a "singles group"
does not *totally* bring about the healing in a single person's life to feel loved, needed, and forgiven.

The good news is, God has a place for each one of us.
"God [sets] the solitary in families." Every day of our
lives, He waits for us to ask Him for the family relationships we so desperately need.

5
My Amazing Kids

"Mom, we need to start going to church," Gloria said. Her voice sounded gentle but very firm, and her sweet face wore a serious, mature look. A few months before, Gloria had turned sixteen. *Instead of the traditional Sweet Sixteen party,* I thought, *her parents divorced each other. How does she stand it?*

"Which church do you want to visit, Mom?" she persisted. "You know we all need it. Nothing will get better for any of us until we start going to church again."

I knew she was right, but church was almost the last place I felt like going. I didn't like some Christians. I didn't like their questions, their judgments, their stares, and their quoting Scriptures to me. I wanted to stay right there in Mama's Oklahoma home, often curled up in bed in that fetal position, crying, and suffering. My shock, exhaustion, and burnout were acute. I simply couldn't face any challenge, even something so basic in my life as Sunday School and church.

Several months earlier, I had arranged to fly with the kids to Selma, Alabama, the home of Bobbie and John Ames, for some much-needed rest and privacy from all the turmoil at home, the controversy, and harassment by the media. My dear friends, Judi Wilson and musical conductor Jack Conner, were God sent to help any way they could. I had whisked the kids to our devoted secretary

Jackie Lee's house to wait until flight time, while I took care of last-minute details. I had asked Charlie Morgan, our family friend and lawyer, to be with Bob when the divorce papers were served. I walked into Jackie's front door just after one of my children had turned on her television—and heard the news flash. I had divorced their father. I found all four kids weeping, totally devastated.

I was devastated as well, and angry with disbelief. It should not have happened that way. I planned to tell them there, in that quiet and neutral place, away from our hectic household. Now even this, the most crucial moment of their innocent lives, had been invaded by the press. The scene was one of turmoil added to heartbreak.

Somehow we got to the plane, and the five of us wept as the aircraft lifted away from Miami and headed toward Alabama. No other hours of my life felt more painful, and for months the most indescribable feelings of failure and worthlessness swept over me whenever I recalled the sight of those despairing young faces. *My children.*

Once this storm blew over, Bobbie Ames returned with us to Miami. Bobbie gave us moral support and helped the children and me to pack our van for a summer visit with Mama and Paw Paw in Mannford, Oklahoma, just outside of Tulsa. Even at Mama's house we seemed to stay in turmoil. I could not hide my exhausted mind, body, and emotions from anyone else. My concerned family tried to tiptoe around so I could rest. Instead of rest, however, I experienced torment: fear, self-condemnation, grief, nausea, a longing to die.

Outwardly OK but emotionally on hold, my kids fished, explored, and tried to enjoy a normal summer. They had no idea what might happen next. Where would we live? Where would they attend school? What would happen to us?

Besides those stresses, my children were frightened for me. I had been their anchor and basically the family breadwinner. They never before had seen me so depressed and crying continually. Now their anchor had failed. Bobby, nearly seventeen, tried to hold the family together, and Gloria, sixteen, tried to minister to me. Barbara and Billy, the twins, at age eleven needed both parents, as did the older kids.

So we continued, each living and reliving his own separate heartbreak, while my mother and stepfather did their best to take care of our family. After three weeks of this, Gloria had enough. I'm sure she probably conferred with Bobby, but she came to me on her own and confronted me about our family's failure to attend church. Her words were low-key and kind, but the unspoken message came through loud and clear. *Enough is enough, Mom. We've got to move on. The pity party is over.*

"You're right, Gloria," I told her. "We'll talk it over and decide. We'll go to church on Sunday."

"Thanks, Mom," was all she said, but her smile was the first real sunshine I had seen on Gloria's face for many long weeks.

How much do our children know or understand? we wonder at such crisis times. From my experience, I'd say it's far more than we adults would guess. At that point, though, I felt sure my kids must have hated me. I had been the erratic parent, the one who traveled and rehearsed, worked at night, and sometimes had an out-of-town booking on someone's birthday and had to postpone the party. Through the years, though, we often traveled all night and made many sacrifices in order to have more time with the children.

However, I was the one too often who was dead tired and impatient, apt to get mad and yell. *Good mothers never lose their self-control,* I thought. *They stay home every day, listen to their children, smile a lot, and always serve them milk and cookies.*

Beyond those negatives, my kids had to put up with the homosexual "rights" issue which exploded around us—with me at the center. There had been strenuous months filled with community meetings, referendums, strategy sessions, news interviews, and people in and out of our house at all hours. My children absorbed a lot of that. They also grew accustomed to hate mail, rumors of my death, cruel Anita Bryant jokes on television, continual bomb threats, and police dogs sniffing for bombs supposedly hidden in our house.

That atmosphere prevailed for fourteen dreadful months. One afternoon the twins rushed in from school with something urgent to tell me. "Some men rolled down the window of their car," Billy said, "and told us, 'We're gonna get your mommie!'"

At that I called all the kids together and told them they were not to fear. "Unless God permitted it, no one could touch even a hair of my head," I assured them. "Do you believe that?"

Each child said he or she *believed* God would protect us. They seemed satisfied with my explanation and seemed unconcerned. Actually, they handled those incredible months—the harassment, stressful home life, questions from schoolmates—extremely well, I thought.

At home, meanwhile, parental arguments began to escalate. The public stand I took *against* a new law favoring homosexuals to have the so-called "right" to teach in a private religious school created a furor. As my personal manager, my husband had worked for years toward a consistent career image for me, successfully guiding my work decisions in some very creative ways. Most Americans seemed to consider me as likable as Mom and apple pie. My visibility level was high, wide, and wholesome.

Bob, at the beginning, believing it was a *local issue,* had agreed, along with our pastor Bill Chapman, that I should attend the Dade County Commission meeting to protest the passing of that ungodly and unnecessary law. Over the years we had worked with many homosexuals, but this law was infringing on our rights as parents to rear and teach our children according to God's principles in pri-

A New Day

vate religious schools. The commissioner who had proposed that ordinance, without my knowledge, was the same one I had helped get elected to office. I was reluctant to go. As a matter of fact, I was terrified at the thought of appearing, for I had never been in a courtroom hearing. However, God Almighty allowed my circumstances to hem me in on every side, so that I had no choice other than to take a stand for the Lord and to protect our children. As it turned out, I then became identified with a national issue that not only was controversial, but ugly. The press called me bigoted, some Christians called me brave, and my husband in his heart called me someone foolish enough to destroy a career he had worked years to help me build.

Bob felt intense anger and vented it toward me verbally, while I, on the other hand, was having a hard enough time with outside pressures. It was *not* the boycotting and blacklisting of my career, but the extreme deterioration inside that did me in. Satan has two tools—deception and accusation—to divide and conquer, and these instruments, combined with stresses too enormous for our weakened marriage to survive, toppled the relationship.

Our children knew that Bob, in his mind's eye, saw me senselessly throwing away our livelihood, while he worked desperately to salvage as much of my career as he could. They also knew when one major sponsor after another called it quits. Many press releases and conferences were strategies by Bob and his staff to proclaim all the job discrimination and blacklisting of Anita Bryant. It was the truth, but this tactic backfired, and instead of creating sympathy, it only drove more fear into the minds and hearts of those business executives (Christian and non-Christian), who were shaky to begin with in their principles, but solid in their love of money. Therefore, it became popular to cancel all contracts with Anita Bryant.

The more my career went down the tubes, the greater the cause became to "Save Our Children." Christians were coming out of the closet against this unconstitutional law as fast as the gays were coming out for it! However, the homosexuals' vicious attacks of intimidation on me to the media, through the mail, phone calls, or demonstrations, eventually took their toll. The yielding of many Christians to threats of militant attacks unwittingly combined to put Anita Bryant "out of business." We lost eighty important bookings within a year, a lucrative network TV show contract with the Singer Sewing Machine Company, and on and on.

The crowning blow came when the Florida Citrus Commission decided to bow out. As their spokeswoman, I had helped them accomplish the most successful sales campaign in advertising history. I loved and admired the citrus growers, most of whom were Christians. At last, however, they decided not to renew my contract; their ad agency had pronounced me "too controversial" by taking a poll at the *height* of the issue. It naturally showed me, at that time, to be as well-known for my stand as for selling Florida orange juice. It's a shame they didn't wait a little for the smoke to clear. Then perhaps they would have seen the mail running ten to one in favor of Anita Bryant, and more people were buying Florida orange juice than homosexuals were boycotting it! The truth was that the ad agency, along with some of the Florida Commission staff, were fed up with the hassle and also with the challenge of having always to be creative for eleven years with their spokesperson. They seized the opportunity to ax me. I share this with no malice in my heart—only to set the record straight as I saw it.

Despite all efforts to shield them, the kids suffered through much of this fallout. At times when their parents' tempers flared, and bitter words and harsh accusations flew, I would see such hurt and dismay on their faces. They were afraid of what might happen. They dreaded the possibility of our divorcing, though they did not hear Bob and me speak of that potential tragedy.

When my career was diminishing, Anita Bryant Ministries was born, and Bob became the president. Meanwhile, I had seen plenty of disillusioning scenarios. At times I had stayed in ministers' homes, and couldn't help seeing deserted and dysfunctional families. I realized that very few clergymen involved themselves or their churches with homosexual issues or ministry to sexually disturbed men and women. And in our own Christian home, there was continuous strife with no real intimacy and constant anxiety. I had nothing left to give, and this understandably infuriated Bob. Clearly we needed to pick up the pieces of our daily lives, but had nothing left with which to do it. We couldn't discuss anything. We did not trust each other.

As our children's apprehensions mounted, they had no one to build them up. They saw too much, heard too much, and received too little comfort from their overworked and overwrought parents.

As for me, I felt I was not a good wife or mother and couldn't hold everything together for even one more day. The marriage went from bad to worse. My desperation was compounded daily. I knew with a horrible certainty that everything must be my fault, yet I could do no more. I was wiped out.

Now, after the fact, it never occurred to me that God would speak to me so directly through my own child. Sure, He had done that before, but Gloria's insistence that we find a church to attend was to become a primary step toward our family's healing. Though I did not want to take that step, I knew my child was right.

That day, dwelling in the horrible black pit of my own misery and degradation, I overlooked two central and permanent facts: Each of my children had his or her individual faith in Jesus Christ, and God had no intention of leaving or deserting any of us, not even me.

Church attendance became our first act of normalcy.

The things I dreaded did not happen. Church services, prayers, altar calls, fellowship with other believers, even the precious old hymns we sang, brought us closer to the Lord on whom we always had depended. There were no overnight miracles, but each of us felt a new beginning.

So we plodded through that soul-scorched summer, each simply putting one foot before the other. Making myself do the "normal" things—church, laundry, cooking dinner, driving the kids to the mall—gradually made life become more nearly normal. My kids needed me, so I made the effort. Without my children, I might not have survived. Becoming a full-fledged mother to my children, often by an act of willpower, helped return me to my basic self.

Bobby, my oldest, always had been especially close to his father. Whenever Bob and I had conflicts, Bobby took on a critical spirit, just like his dad. Since the other kids looked up to their big brother, I felt certain that all four blamed me for the divorce. I feared that Bobby would decide to stay with his father, and probably Gloria would make the same choice. Such thoughts felt like a kick in the stomach.

That day on the plane to Alabama, as each of us cried, I felt more love for Bobby than for myself. "I love you enough to free you to make your own decision," I told him.

"I appreciate your giving me that freedom," he replied, even as I wept to think of having to surrender my son. *Bobby has the hardest time of all,* I thought, and it broke my heart that my tall son had to undertake the man-sized task of making such a grievous decision about his life.

The courts insist that in a divorce, a fourteen-year-old has to make the decision about which parent they will live with. After initially going to Oklahoma with me, Bobby later decided to stay with his dad in Miami and finish high school. Gloria decided to stay with me and the twins in Oklahoma. Bobby and Gloria were understandably angry, confused, and guilt ridden at the same time with both their dad and me. I know firsthand from living in a divorced home that children often feel guilty of somehow helping to create the situation. For not always obeying their parents and not being "perfect," they become loaded with guilt feelings. There is no question it is never the children's fault, and this was certainly the case with our children, but there is no way to avoid or control these feelings in a child. It was tearing my insides out, yet in my heart I had to free them so they could make the right decisions. All I could do was pray that the Lord would break through all the darkness over them and let "His light" pierce through to their hearts and minds. I had at least been faithful to lead my children to Jesus in their young years, and I trusted He would lead them through this painful experience. God was faithful to my children.

As time passed, the kids and I learned more and more about one another. I relished my first opportunity to serve as a full-time mother, and despite our difficult circumstances they seemed to enjoy it, too. After eleven months we moved to Selma, where they enrolled in Dallas Christian Academy, a small Christian private school which teaches students how to live and learn from godly principles. It was not an easy time for them, but they took to small town life like ducks to water. Here was a place with no press conferences, no limousines, no pushy strangers . . . and you could ride your bike to school. We enjoyed those benefits. I had fun growing tomatoes in the back yard, and trying my luck with zinnias and petunias as well. The kids could wander anywhere in perfect safety, and nobody taunted them.

One day in nearby Birmingham, however, Barbara and I discovered that the old nightmares still lurked, even in a harmless-appearing shopping mall. We had just purchased her new shoes and stood waiting for my change, when the bombshell dropped. The saleswoman recognized me, and she had a question.

"Scripturally, what makes it right for you to be remarried? I'm divorced because my husband left me. Was your divorce scriptural? How can you justify this? What gives you the right?"

I felt as though the ground was sliding from under my feet, but I figured where her questions originated. One of the scandal sheets had reported that I was engaged. What should I say? While I fought back tears and angry feelings, literally biting my tongue to hold back some words I didn't want to say, my little Barbara stepped forward and saved the situation.

"You don't know my mother," she stated quietly, her green eyes blazing. "You don't know the pain she has suffered. How can you judge her?"

That was all. The incident was over. I felt so proud of Barbara, and was so shocked at her mature response, that I reacted in quite the opposite way from her behavior. I cried.

That same scene happened many times, and it always hurt. When I thought of my daughter defending me, however, much of the pain would disappear.

Billy, my happy-go-lucky son, possesses the great gift of being able to make the best of most any circumstances. He is a gifted artist, but his real art is his good nature, his kidding, and sometimes an unexpected streak of sensitivity toward poor old Mom. Bill's the one who could drive his twin crazy all day, then confide to an adult family friend that he wished Barbara would get serious about her singing. "I believe in her talent," he said.

Those days I saw that my children's lives certainly were not always easy. Their standard of living changed drastically as my income dried up and I began selling my assets. They could not always have things they needed or wanted, and I hated not being able to buy them whatever I wanted them to have.

Billy found me crying one day when the financial picture looked really bleak. "What's wrong, Mom?" he asked, his face full of adolescent concern. I began to list all my woes as he listened, full of sympathy. When I finished, he asked, gently, "But Mom, . . . where is your faith?"

That tiny rebuke jerked my spine up straight. I dried my tears and told Billy, "You are right. Faith is our answer." Then I had a private chuckle with God over His choice of a prophet for me that day—one who was barefoot, dressed in ragged cutoff jeans, with his hair pulled back into a skimpy ponytail. "Lord, You sure have a sense of humor," I sighed.

So began the education of Mom. "I always hated it that we had so many toys," Bobby told me one day. "It embarrassed me to have so much more than other kids."

"Me too," Gloria chimed in. They weren't criticizing me, only explaining. They knew I loved to buy presents for my children because I had grown up in a family that had lots of love, but little cash.

For my part, I had to crack down on the kids and get them serious about their lives. Grades slipped following the divorce, as you would expect. As a full-time mother, and father, I needed to install house rules and make them stick. Homework, piano practice, allowances, clean rooms—soon I realized I felt more like a referee than a mother. It seemed I was continually following up on someone, or telling one person or another to stop bickering or sassing, or to turn down the stereo.

Sometimes it got so nerve-wracking that I'd stop giving verbal instructions and post notes on the doors of their rooms. One day I stood in the hall and counted the little pink notes pasted on Barbara's door, then Billy's, when the doors opened, and the kids came out and saw what I was doing. We laughed so hard that all discipline was lost.

Yet, something was emerging from all that chaos. Because I felt little self-confidence in my mothering skills, I continually found myself on my knees before God. Every day I lifted each child to God in prayer and oftentimes several times a day would pray for special needs. We often prayed together one-on-one before a dreaded test or a school skit. Prayers became natural and habitual, and my kids and I saw God's answers.

God honors a mother's prayers. I began to understand that God wants our faithfulness, and doesn't expect us to be the supermom we don't know how to be. I also perceived that my children always had known me and accepted me exactly as I am.

"Mom never gives herself credit for being a good mother because she is a professional singer," Barbara explained to a family friend. "She wanted to be like other people's mothers, and she doesn't understand that we want her to be like she is.

"She's a good singer _and_ a good mother," my daughter said. As usual with Barbara, her thoughts amazed me. I had no idea she felt that way.

Divorce, like any other major crisis, seems to draw a line between who you were and who you will be. Struggling with this, we inevitably begin to collide with the child we once were. The pain and anguish of divorce resonates with the fears and misunderstandings of our early life, and unless we are careful, we can transfer much of this emotional baggage to our children.

That was true for me. I eventually decided to begin Christian counseling with prayerfully chosen, accredited individuals who ministered through prayer and counseling, as led by God's Holy Spirit. Those sessions illuminated some long-standing hurts and unresolved conflicts and allowed me, with God's help, to deal with past traumas and put most of them to rest.

It was not easy. It is hard to dredge up the garbage of life and look at it. There is much emotional pain. One issue which had to be dealt with was something I had blocked from my thinking during all my adult life. Sexual abuse.

There had been three incidents during my grammar-school years, and as an adolescent I experienced a long period of abuse by an adult authority figure, but not a family member. Later, in my thirties, I confronted that hidden, angry memory with help from a friend, and through Jesus Christ, forgave him. That action, I thought, would banish the awful memories and emotions that lingered on inside me, but it didn't work that way. My debilitating feelings of anger, shame and guilt (I assumed these episodes happened because somehow I caused them) continued to fester within me.

The right kind of Christian counseling enabled me to understand the truth. The feelings of shame and worthlessness deep inside me at last could be resolved. I also came to realize that running from such unbearable emotional traps had led me, unhealed, into the supposed safety net of youthful marriage.

According to statistics, one girl in every four experiences sexual abuse, and one boy in five. Those children need help to handle the complex emotional damage which results. Only now, years into my Christian walk, can I at last acknowledge that I was one of the children who experienced those terrible things.

One last footnote: Several women I know came to Selma for a James Robison revival crusade, and piled into my house to spend the night. Dressed in our nighties and robes, we curled up on my big bed to talk, laugh, and eat ice cream like a bunch of overgrown college girls.

When someone mentioned childhood sexual abuse, the conversation abruptly changed. Shyly, reluctantly, one after another admitted it had happened to them. Four of the five beautiful Christian women in my house had been abused during their childhood! For three of us, it marked the first time we could bring ourselves to tell another person.

Counseling with skilled Christian professionals helps us deal with emotional loads too heavy for us to carry. With our eyes fixed on Jesus Christ, remembering His words, "My yoke is easy and my burden is light" (Matt. 11:30), we begin to experience the peace of God that passes all understanding. We begin to love ourselves to the extent that we can now accept His love for us.

When God provides us with courage to deal with a conflicted past, we gratefully realize that such horrors need not affect our children. Inadequate to deal with my own painful emotions, I knew I was powerless to meet my children's equally deep needs. We could and did pray, however, and they saw me become willing to tackle my own confused emotions. They respected that. We all eventually went through Christian counseling together and experienced some deep healing in our family relationships.

Once when Gloria accompanied me to a television talk show where I made a guest appearance, the interviewer surprised my daughter with a tough question: How did your parents' divorce affect you? Gloria is very poised and also very honest. I had no idea what she might say.

"When Mom gave up show business, that decision changed my life," Gloria replied. She said, "I had yearned to spend more time with Mom. My mother's Christian testimony formed the foundation of our mother-daughter relationship, and my parents' divorce forced each of us to test our faith in God and in one another." Her response touched me so, and I was proud of her.

Remembering that decimated woman who curled up in bed at Mama's house, terrified that she had ruined the lives she loved the most, I realized God had provided at Calvary everything that broken person ever would need. I think of the messenger the Lord sent to that failing mother: her daughter, who pointed the mother toward the helps she desperately needed—church, God's altar, our starting place.

Not every child in today's shattered world finds protection from the terrors of modern life. Parents divorce.

They abuse drugs, alcohol, and each other. There are too many dysfunctional homes, far too many alienated and suffering sons and daughters.

There are precious opportunities of childhood—a time for direction, correction and, most of all, protection. Harried and overworked as today's women often are, nevertheless, we must return to committed motherhood. God has called us to awesome responsibilities, and too often we fail Him.

Somers White, president of a Phoenix, Arizona, management and financial consulting company and a noted public speaker, likes to distribute copies of a "Letter from a Boy Just Released from Prison":

"Dear Folks:

"Thank you for everything, but I am going to Chicago and try to start some kind of new life.

"You asked me why I did those things and why I gave you so much trouble, and the answer is easy for me to give you, but I am wondering if you will understand.

"Remember when I was about six or seven and I used to want you to just listen to me? I remember all the nice things you gave me for Christmas and my birthday and I was real happy with the things for about a week, but the rest of the year I really didn't want presents. I just wanted all the time for you to listen to me like I was somebody who felt things too, because I remember even when I was young I felt things. But you said you were too busy.

"Mom, you are a wonderful cook and you had everything so clean and you were so tired so much from doing all those things that made you busy, but you know something, Mom? I would have liked crackers and peanut butter just as well—if you had only sat down with me and said to me, 'Tell me all about it so I can maybe help you understand.'

"And when Donna came I couldn't understand why

everybody made so much fuss, because I didn't think it was my fault that her hair is curly and her teeth so white and she doesn't have to wear glasses with such thick lenses. Her grades were better too, weren't they?

"If Donna ever has children, I hope you will tell her to just pay some attention to the one that doesn't smile very much, because that one will be really crying inside. And when she's about to bake six dozen cookies to make sure first that the kids don't want to tell her about a dream or a hope or something because thoughts are important, too, to small kids, even though they don't have so many words to use when they tell about what they have inside them.

"I think all the kids who are doing so many things that the grownups are tearing their hair out or worrying about are really looking for somebody that will have the time to listen a few minutes and who really and truly will treat them as they would a grownup who might be useful to them. If you folks had ever said to me, 'Pardon me,' when you interrupted me, I'd have dropped dead. If anybody asks you where I am, tell them I have gone looking for somebody with time, because I've got a lot of things I want to talk about.

Love to all,
Your son"

That letter says it all. The boy who wrote it could have been my child, or yours; for sure, he is God's child. May our Heavenly Father help us rescue our children from the evils of this world, and from the mistakes even loving parents can inflict.

Jesus said, "Feed my lambs" (John 21:15).

Though we believe ourselves incapable, we still must try. For the sake of America, for the sake of God's kingdom, may we women return to the job of nurturing and men return to loving and leading their families.

May God help each of us to mother and father and to

help sustain the world's most wonderful kids—your kids, mine, the baby-sitter, the boy who delivers pizza, the pregnant teenager, the kid in jail—each one precious in His sight.

May children lead their mothers and fathers to Your altar, Lord. There, You will revive us again.

6
Friends and Other Angels

"What about your wardrobe?" Bonnie asked me.

"I don't know."

"Anita, hosting a national television show like Pat Robertson's '700 Club' for a whole week means you have to update your clothes. Do you have what you need to do this job?"

"Well . . ."

Naturally Bonnie Brosius, an Atlanta fashion designer who operates two boutiques (Chabar) in upscale locales (I had met her when we moved to Atlanta) immediately would think about clothes. Her custom pieces look fabulous—simple, elegant, striking, as straightforward as the designer. Now she stood before me, a determined look on her pretty face, and confronted my need.

"Let's make a deal. I'll travel with you that week and be your wardrobe mistress. We'll put your clothes together."

"But Bonnie, how can I pay you?"

"You can repay me some other way," she said firmly. "Anita, you need to learn how to barter."

Knowing Bonnie Brosius was like taking a course in Friendship 101, I thought. Our paths happened to cross soon after the kids and I moved to Atlanta, where we knew few people. I made the move for career reasons. By then I had been single for five years and had become used to coping with the many challenges single women face: driver's licenses for two kids, plus long-distance chauffeuring for their drivers education classes; my oldest girl Gloria, a college graduate now, back living with me and working; finding affordable housing and schools; running a household; earning a living—you are familiar with the list.

With all that, who can afford the luxury of friendships? Where would I find time?

Bonnie, I discovered, struggled with those same problems and perhaps a few more. Also divorced, Christian, and a woman with four children who had suffered severe rejection as well as physical and emotional pain, Bonnie looked as fragile as a Christmas-tree angel, but could work like a horse. She has great inner strength and a determination to follow Jesus. I saw she meant business about living out her faith.

We made time for friendship. Here was another "one-woman band," someone who taught herself to design, purchase fabrics, cut, sew, merchandise, and run a business—and did much of that solo. Though Bonnie was a newcomer to the fashion scene, she recognized her talent and was willing to bet on herself. She was exactly the kind of model God knew I needed, and I know He directed our friendship.

Bonnie sustained me in certain ways, I sustained her in others. We developed a give-and-take relationship that became as sturdy and dependable as a towering oak tree. And gradually, Bonnie taught me one of the most important lessons of my life; although I had been going through this painful class since my divorce, she taught me to receive.

Like many other performers, I never had enough time for many in-depth relationships. Travel, work, upgrading professional skills, enlarging my repertoire and maintaining the physical level needed to do such strenuous work—added to the pressing needs of husband, children, and home—left precious little time even to know myself, much less others.

All my adult life, I longed for day-to-day friendships like other women enjoy. Instead of lunches or tennis dates with other women, however, I had to work with my music arranger, vocalize, or perhaps study terms of an upcoming concert booking. The schedule never quit. It owned me. Rarely could I steal time to do anything purely for pleasure. If I went shopping or to a movie I felt guilty.

Once on my own, though, with those relentless career pressures behind me, at last I could form the friendships I had always yearned to enjoy. The problem was, I didn't always understand the ground rules.

For example, I've always enjoyed giving—everything from gag gifts, important gifts, parties, wonderful food, flowers and more flowers, you name it. Taking, however, was pretty much outside my experience. Now here was Bonnie, wanting me to accept items I could not afford to buy, extending herself when matters were as tough for her as they were for me.

Through Bonnie, I learned to receive. As she explained, friendship involves giving *and* receiving, and where you have just one side of that equation, you have a lopsided friendship. That seemed easy to say but hard to compute. I realize now that learning to receive from friends, *humbling* yourself, not having to occupy the driver's seat in the relationship, are essential lessons.

Even our Lord Jesus Christ humbled Himself to receive His human needs from the hands of ordinary people around Him. He had "no place to lay His head" (see Matt. 8:20; Luke 9:58), and His followers and friends—including many devout women—provided Him with food, hospitality, and lodging.

So here is Bonnie, a dynamite blonde who turns heads when she enters a room, but, more importantly, she is a radiant, practicing Christian. As time went on we bailed each other out a hundred times. She put gas in my car; I put gas in hers. We shared. We cried together, prayed together, complained together, and asked God a million times what was wrong with us. Why couldn't we get our acts together? Why weren't we successfully married? It turned out much later that the Lord answered our prayers for "His choice" of husbands. I had lunch with Cliff Flood, a tall handsome, airline pilot from Oklahoma, later introduced him to Bonnie, and never dated him again. I teased them both unmercifully as I wished them well at their wedding reception. Her joy was mine!

Without Bonnie and Charlotte Smith and some others, I never would have made it. Charlotte and I had been neighbors in Miami Beach years earlier, where I had the privilege of leading her in the sinner's prayer, and into a commitment to Jesus Christ. Her then terminally ailing husband, well-known business magnate Dan Topping, plus all five children, came to the Lord as a result. Now my circumstances had drastically changed, but my friend stuck by me. Once when she offered help and I felt that old pride rise up, she said something unforgettable. "What you did for me I could never repay," she said quietly, "because it has eternal value." Through her example, this gracious, dear friend taught me much about giving as "unto the Lord." The ten years of my "wilderness" journey as a single humbled me to a point of receiving many times, and Charlotte was always there for me.

Such friendships support us during the best of times and the worst of times; they strengthen us every day of our lives. Without such open, giving Christian relationships, how could any of us stand during periods when the bottom seems to drop out of our lives?

It distresses me to see how many people suffer from loneliness and alienation. Stresses and pressures of daily life seem to rob men and women of time for the upbuilding and affirmations others can give them. I received a letter from a pastor's wife who described this dilemma sensitively.

"I wish I had a close friend," she wrote. "As a pastor's wife I'm not really allowed the luxury. The only people I know are members of the church. When I talk to them I always have to be careful of what I say. I have to watch how I speak of John (not his real name).

"I don't have anyone I can go to, to talk about my problems. I can't talk to church members because it might lessen their opinion of John. In a small way, I am in the public eye too. I feel like I'm walking on eggshells.

"Where do I turn? Where can I find a friend, someone I can talk to or ask for help?"

This chapter is written to individuals like this woman, people who, like me, find their hearts crying out for simple, ordinary, soul-satisfying companionship. I truly related to that letter writer's feelings. Like her, I have had times when I desperately yearned for the intimacy you feel toward another person who knows exactly what you are but doesn't judge, criticize, or correct you except in love, and who forgives you when you blunder.

Teddy Heard, my once-in-a-lifetime friend in Houston, fit that description. I could tell Teddy anything; my imperfections never seemed to shock her. Spiritually mature and vibrant in her adventurous Christian walk, Teddy taught me a lot about Christian freedom. Hers was a marvelously free spirit, largely because she accepted others exactly the way they are—just as Jesus does.

When Teddy Heard went to be with the Lord at age thirty-nine, I had lost an irreplaceable friendship. She was the first close friend to teach me about death, and for months I was overwhelmed with grief. Teddy had taught me well, however. One day I realized that my spirit would tell me that she really hadn't left me at all. "I'm right here, Sugar," I could imagine hearing her say in that wonderful Texas drawl, "Just next door with the Lord. You and I will always be friends. We haven't lost a thing!"

You can imagine my shock, then, when in Nashville—fifteen years after Teddy left us—she seemed to walk through my front door. Of course it was "little Teddy," her oldest daughter, all grown up now, a tall beauty with her mother's dark hair, deep dimples, and infectious laugh. We had a joyous reunion, and I praised God for His reuniting me with my precious friend in this special way.

Yes, Teddy Heard continues to give to me. Sometimes when I get in a jam, I think, *What would Teddy say?* Then I know what to say and do. She also left me a legacy of so many great attitudes. She saw Christ in all sorts of people, and like Him, saw potential in people others didn't bother with—angry people, alcoholics, panhandlers, "bad" teenagers, men and women whose lives seemed frozen in permanent disappointments.

"People are so worth knowing," she'd say. "Jesus cares about every one of us!"

Because of Teddy, I made it a point to try to enjoy many different people, not just those I considered "my type." Needless to say, this makes life richer and more interesting, but at times much more painful.

Many times, I noticed, single adults won't take time to make friendships with those of the opposite sex. They want to date, but can't be bothered to entertain another person just as a friend and not a potential marriage partner. Teddy would not have made that mistake. Like her, I decided to enjoy older people, younger people, people in professions far different from mine, and, most of all, those who make me feel good, those who help me to laugh.

People you can cry with, laugh with, or pray with keep you in touch with reality. I cherish such friends.

Whenever I felt really alone and bereft in my new life as a single woman, God almost always showed me a friend I wasn't aware I had. A letter would arrive from someone I had never met: "When you were under fire and I heard reports on TV, I wept for you and prayed. When the reports quit coming, and there was such a long silence, I would remember you and pray. You had a part in my finding Christ, and your lovely singing still inspires me. I love you, beautiful lady. . . ."

Alone? Do we really think we are or have to be alone? God leads people to others, according to His divine plan, by mail, telephone, or what we think is accident. "Are you *the* Anita Bryant?" people sometimes asked me.

"If you like me, I am," I'd tell them. "If you don't, I'm not." I wasn't altogether joking, either. Sometimes the nicest-looking people would light into me and almost annihilate me. Someone once observed that the Christian army is the only one that kills its wounded. For a while, I almost believed that.

Eventually I allowed the Lord to help me relax and enjoy new people, laugh and kid with them, without wondering if they loved me or despised me. I marveled at how many *strangers* (what an impersonal word!) went out of their way to offer friendship, kind thoughts, and amazing encouragement.

I met a classmate at our high-school reunion, for example, and while waiting in the airport for his flight home to his wife and family, he took time to write me a note. He cared enough to encourage me.

Beth Bazemore, a Florida friend with a nearly blind friend who writes poems, sent one of these to me. I will share it with you. Such notes, letters, and poems seemed to arrive at the exact moment that I needed God's touch. God sent friends and other angels to minister to me, and He will do the same for you.

The poem Beth sent me expresses that same thought—that "there is a friend that sticketh closer than a brother" (Prov. 18:24). That Friend is Jesus Christ.

He Was There
(Exodus 33:14)

Jesus heard when you prayed last night,
   He talked with God about you;
Jesus was there when you fought that fight,
   He is going to bring you through.

Jesus knew when you shed those tears,
  But you did not weep alone;
For the burden you thought too heavy to bear,
  He made His very own.

Jesus Himself was touched by that trial,
  Which you could not understand;
Jesus stood by as you almost fell,
  And lovingly grasped your hand.

Jesus cared when you bore that pain;
  Indeed, He bore it too;
He felt each pang, each ache in your heart,
  Because of His love for you.

Jesus was grieved when you doubted His love,
  But He gave you grace to go on;
Jesus rejoiced as you trusted Him
  The only trustworthy one.

His presence shall ever be with you,
  No need to be anxious or fret;
Wonderful Lord! He was there all the time,
  He has never forsaken you yet.

Sometimes God even sends the friend of a friend to supply your specific need. That happened to me when I met Ann Platz, introduced by another friend, Charlotte Hale, after we moved to Atlanta.

Ann is a Christian and a noted interior designer. It didn't surprise me that she was interested in the town house I had leased, and asked many questions about it. But I felt flabbergasted when Ann said, "I think God told me to help you put your house together."

Elated as I felt, that kind of service wasn't in my budget. Besides, our furniture was crowded into a much smaller house than the one we had left. I didn't see how anyone could make it look like anything. "Let me try," Ann said. I can't tell you how grateful I felt.

I told our mutual friend to make sure Ann understood that I couldn't buy draperies and other furnishings just then. But as Ann moved furniture about, our rooms began to look dramatically different. As she placed pictures on the wall, moved accessories from one place to a better one, and hung mirrors to add visual depth and reflect beautiful views, I began to understand what God was doing.

"The Lord wants you to love your home, and to make a good place for you and your children," Ann told me. "You don't need to spend much money. God gave you virtually everything you need for this house many years ago! Now all we have to do is arrange and refine what you have."

Though she had just met me, it was as though Ann intuitively understood me and my family. Soon our house looked as though we had lived there for years. It glowed and sparkled. Favorite things had their special places. We could find our way around in the dark. "Thank You, Lord," I prayed. "You see how important it is for me to feel at home."

So it went. God sent people into my life in the most incredible ways, people who changed my life far more than they will ever imagine. During this time, when I so often felt alone and powerless, I learned to pray God would send new friends into my life. Why don't we pray that more often? Is there anyone in the world who has too many friends?

Kenny Rogers and his wife Mary Ann especially encouraged me, and both took time out of their busy schedules to be friends and to give me career advice. Dick Clark, of "American Band Stand," related to me in the pain of divorce and wrote me a sweet note. He also later had the courage to have me perform on a television special in the late 70s, in spite of opposition.

I also learned to pray for healthy relationships. For example, I noticed sometimes when I had dinner with a nice man we'd spend the evening with him reciting all the negatives about his failed marriage, ex-girlfriend, and the like. Why dwell on the past? Why not accept a new friendship as a new gift, and not drag old baggage into it first thing?

Of course, we need to care for one another and share one another's burdens. Yet, every relationship need not turn into an amateur therapy session, advice marathon, or pity party. I learned to ask God for mature, give-and-take relationships.

I also promised God that I would stay away from "poor-me clubs," wherein we dwell on our difficulties, failures, and past mistakes. We all experience failure, and God wants us to care when our brother stumbles. But when my own life bottomed out, I did not want friends to get down in the pit with me (Jesus already was there), but to stretch out their hands and help lift me out.

Too much sympathy and empathy can help us cripple ourselves. True friends sometimes have to give tough love. Paul wrote about "Speaking the truth in love" (Eph. 4:15), which is not always easy, but is the loving thing to do.

Friendship not only prevents us from succumbing to a self-centered life-style, but helps balance our lives. I realize that I need the daily discipline of offering myself in friendship. I truly want to appreciate other people, and learn how to show it.

When Teddy Heard was transformed from this life into the next, some seven thousand people attended her services. I sang "How Great Thou Art." Standing before that huge number of friends who loved her, I remembered the day I asked her how she found time to maintain her huge circle of friendships.

"Mama taught me something she also taught her Baptist Sunday School class," she laughed. "J-O-Y! Jesus first, others second, yourself last of all."

Teddy was intimately in touch with joy. She used that little formula to fill her life to overflowing. Teddy was one of the many angels the Lord has sent into my life. Sometimes when our lives crumble, and we feel as though we don't deserve anything beyond failure and trials, at that very moment He sends a friend for us to love forever.

Our part is to open our hearts and let that person come in. God will do the rest.

7
Making New Moves

or years, whenever I autographed one of my
books or albums, I scrawled one special
Scripture verse above my signature: "I can
do all things through Christ, which strengtheneth me"
(Phil. 4:13).

That was "my" Scripture, the verse I stood on, leaned
upon, and clung to during those dizzying years when my
career obligations escalated madly. "All things," to me,
stood for the unremitting professional schedule which
moved so fast that often I hardly unpacked from one engagement before plunging into the next big challenge.

"All things" meant the difficulties of putting husband,
children, and home ahead of the never-ending rehearsals,
wardrobe fittings, recording sessions, writing books, media interviews, and hundreds of other details. Most of all,
it meant the determination to put God first every day.
Otherwise, I might not meet with Him at all, and that day,
for spiritual purposes, would be lost.

I well learned, however, that whenever I put Jesus first,
"I can do all things through Christ" proved positively
true. I also learned to discipline myself to crawl out of
bed earlier and make time for prayer, Bible reading, and
conversations with God before each hectic day began.

Those days, I often wondered how I possibly could accomplish all I had to do. I dreaded the travel, concert appearances, TV specials, and other enormously demanding
jobs—then felt deep guilt about having such feelings in

the face of God's continual blessings to our family. My emotions alternated between guilt and gratitude. I felt a strong love/hate relationship with my career, often longing to be *just* a mother, *just* a housewife who mopped her own kitchen, and *just* a young woman in blue jeans who sat on the floor with the other women at somebody's prayer group.

I wished I could buy groceries without being recognized, so I wouldn't have to be picture perfect all the time. The idea of having enough time of my own, quality time, to study God's Word and grow into personal maturity, was my idea of utmost luxury. Carrying the ultimate responsibility for our family's welfare often made me feel suffocated and trapped in my own success—success that seldom let me off the treadmill. Though outwardly I appeared confident, inwardly there was a trembling, frightened little girl.

At times like those, I asked God to forgive my selfish feelings. I believe that success comes from God, if it's in His will. Yes, the Lord had blessed me mightily. Not only did we enjoy material security because of His goodness to us, but we received gifts with eternal consequences—our children's salvation, the privilege of leading others to the Lord, and opportunities to witness in churches, in my books, and in the press.

Why, then, did I so often battle depression? At such times, I repeated "my" Scripture: "I can do *all things* through *Christ* who strengtheneth me" (author's italics). That verse is engraved in my brain. It saw me through the most fearful challenges of my life. It helped me relinquish my twin babies to God when they were born prematurely, so tiny and weak doctors feared that neither could survive. (I had come close to death giving them birth.) It helped me sing at my Grandpa and Grandma Berry's funerals. I indeed knew those powerful words and believed them with all my heart.

During that 1980 summer of suffering, even though I

was with the home folks in Oklahoma, it seemed I had no power whatever of my own. Philippians 4:13 did not spring to my mind or my lips as it once had done. Few people wanted my autograph, so I did not write the words. Yes, I still knew the power of God and still believed His truths, but something held us apart. I walked the Christian walk, but at a slight distance. Though I still placed all my confidence in God, I lacked confidence in myself.

Toward summer's end, something nudged me toward making my first move away from Mama, Daddy George, and the rest of my supportive family. Gordona Duca, my girlfriend from Will Rogers High School days, lived just a few houses from us, and she probably brought me to the point of decision.

Gordona had become a high-powered Tulsa real-estate executive, one of America's top salespeople in her profession as CEO of Gordona Duca Realty. For some reason, she insisted on treating me as if I were capable of making surefire decisions and pulling off successful deals just as easily as she did.

Without my realizing what she was doing, Gordona became almost a full-time catalyst for me. "Sure you can, Anita," she'd encourage, when I let my fears pour out and wondered what in the world we'd do next, and if I could manage to do it. *Unlike me,* I thought, *Gordona knew little about failure in the business world. She didn't understand the paralysis that brought one's life to a standstill.*

What's more, she surely didn't recognize that I had almost no savvy about managing money, and had no idea of how to learn. My smart, devoted friend simply was aware I had earned goodly sums in the past, spent a lot, and given much away. I found it hard to make her understand that all those years I had little idea of how our good fortune happened: I merely learned my songs, memorized my lines, and knocked myself out to stay prepared and do my best. The rest somehow followed.

With Gordona's help, and that of others, I began to stand again. My Aunt Betty and Uncle Bob Callen were always available to help, as well as their daughter Cindy and son Rodney. It seemed urgently important to decide where to go and what I must do. Gordona knew that the more often I visited my friends in Selma, Alabama, the more I seemed drawn to that old-timey small town, yet I kept postponing a decision.

At last, she confronted me. "Why are you so afraid to move?"

"Gordona, you make decisions all the time, but I never did it before. My life was decided for me. No wonder I can't . . . ." I began defensively.

"Then, let's get to work right now," Gordona said firmly. "Get some paper and begin listing the pros and cons. If you do decide to move, I guarantee you can do it!"

That is how Gordona Duca walked me through the mental and physical steps necessary to move, pack, locate a home, arrange financing, and all the other details I never before had tackled. With the help of Gordona, I began once more to believe, "I can do all things through Christ."

We did it. By September of that year we had bought a home, chosen good schools, and joined a church. The pastor Von McQueen, his wife Marydell, and several families like Bill and Amelia Jones became precious to us. My emotional state fluctuated from abject fear and depression to occasional self-confidence and joy, and we experienced bad days and good. We had transplanted ourselves and were determined to thrive. Thank God, the kids did just fine. I was the iffy one.

My attitudes often made the situation seem difficult. We had moved to Selma to begin a new life, and I wanted to be left alone to do it. Perversely, however, I complained of loneliness. I longed to experience fully abundant life, yet demanded my privacy. Such contradictions indicate culture shock—not at all unusual, I was to learn, following the trauma of divorce.

For example, some days I felt energetic and cleaned our house from top to bottom. Another time, I might burst into tears because I had to choose the breakfast-room wallpaper. That would plunge me into self-condemnation and despair when I should have let up on myself for a bit. Deep emotional wounds require time to heal: I did not understand that this, too, would pass.

It is vital to realize that God sticks as close to us during the push-and-pull times as He does when we think we have things pretty well together. He never moves or changes. We are the ones who move.

I believed this intellectually, but my feelings did not always obey my convictions. Sometimes my prayers seemed so puny they hardly seemed worth the effort, yet I had faith He heard them and answered. And so, stumbling like a baby, we learn to stand—then walk, again.

I wish everyone could experience the sweetness of life in a small town like Selma, although it can have a down side, too. We felt so unhurried, protected, and comforted there, and immediately appreciated the old-fashioned values and good-hearted people who made the town what it is. Physically, Selma has an indescribable charm—a mix of rural South, with green fields, pickup trucks, and interesting barns, and also the appeal of a sophisticated, very mannerly city life-style.

I loved how people crushed mint from their gardens into tall glasses of iced tea, sat in cushioned porch swings in late afternoon, or worked their flower beds. These were the vignettes you glimpsed whenever you rode through town, especially in the elegantly restored Victorian district. I loved it all.

Slowly, I began to relax. I felt I never would join the rat

race again. Somehow, I must make a living, but not as a singer. Never again, thank God, would I appear in public professionally, or take a stand on anything.

Best of all, the press would never find me in Selma. Media people would not trouble themselves to make the hour-long drive from Birmingham or Montgomery. What's more, no one in Selma cared about my celebrity status, or that my name had been printed in virtually every newspaper and magazine in America. The fact that *Good Housekeeping* magazine had named Anita Bryant number one among America's most admired women for three years running mattered far less to people in Selma than the fact that we attended church and tried to be good neighbors. I liked that.

Early on, I became friends with Gloria Crump, a Selma businesswoman who, like Gordona Duca, took time to encourage and help me. Energetic Gloria, with two other local women, decided to open a fashion boutique in a charming old restored house, and invited me to enter their partnership. *Perfect,* I thought. *Who likes beautiful clothes more than I?* Also, I believed I was conversant with the subject!

Despite strong objections from several males, mostly husbands of my girl friends, I decided to become a partner in The Wardrobe. Since I knew nothing about business, I probably should have heeded all that good advice. My instincts told me this could be an excellent move, and, as it turned out, I was right.

Soon I found myself traveling to Atlanta to undertake the part of my new job I felt sure would be the most fun, selecting and buying the next season's styles at the vast Atlanta Merchandise Mart. With Gloria Crump as my guide, I soon learned my way around that bewildering place. Gloria and her mother had operated a furniture business for years, so she confidently introduced me to the intricacies of buying. *Exhausting work,* I thought, *but what fun!*

Jumping into something new and trying to learn everything at once is not the best way to get your confused life straightened out, but I liked it. Energy began to return, and so did a little self-confidence. Working at The Wardrobe helped me meet many wonderful women. One day, busy at The Wardrobe, a sudden thought occurred to me: *Had I really moved to Selma so I could hide?*

None of my efforts came easily, however. I also had begun to "date," and it felt strange indeed. Luckily, a group of friends had begun to form around me—all sorts of people—professional, married, unmarried, nonworking, career oriented, a real mix. For the first time since high school I could enjoy an uncomplicated pizza date as easily as dinner at the country club. Every time I made myself do new things or meet new people the effort proved rewarding.

The kids and I entered into much healing, adjusting, and accepting our full, new lives. Though at times circumstances still seemed difficult, even painful, people in Selma provided the decent, caring climate in which God wanted us to live. Time and again our neighbors' hands were extended to us in acts of love—offerings simple as a casserole or a bunch of cut flowers, or important as banking advice or help with remodeling our carport.

We all felt a need to give back to the community. I had fallen in love with our town, and wanted to do my part. Larry Striplin, a local industrialist who provided dynamic civic leadership for his hometown and had become our good friend, coaxed me into being involved with a drive to turn the old Walton Theater into a performing-arts center—quite an ambitious goal for a town the size of Selma.

They were able to talk me into it. We decided to stage the kind of star-studded extravaganza you'd expect to find in Atlanta, Detroit, Nashville, or LA, and guess who was appointed chairman?

Once again, God guided even this apparently off-the-wall event in my life, a happening that soon mushroomed far beyond my comfort zone. I immediately contacted Bob Hope, my old warhorse buddy from the days I had joined Bob for seven of his famous U.S.O. tours to entertain U.S. servicemen and women who were overseas at Christmastime. Bob responded to my S.O.S. with his usual gallantry. "I owe you, Anita," he said. "You helped me with that benefit performance in Florida, so I'll gladly help you now." I could have kissed him!

TV and radio spots were made by Bob Hope, and I did some as well as interviews for radio and TV stations within a 100-mile radius of Selma, along with visiting every civic club and church group I could find. It was an exhausting but exhilarating experience!

I talked to God *often* during those several months. My board members worked tirelessly, and most of Selma's leaders (black and white), plus many town folk, volunteered to get the job done. I reminded Him daily that I'd gone out far deeper than I should have. I doubted that I was in good voice anymore, and besides, what was I thinking when I agreed to help produce this white elephant? I'm not a producer! Then came the agonies of trying to pull an extravaganza together—logistics of bringing entertainers into out-of-the-way Selma—expenses, a million details, and, finally, the nagging worry: What if nobody comes?

On Monday, October 24, 1983, "Stars Fell on Alabama" played to a packed stadium of 6,000 wildly enthusiastic fans. The cast included our MC for the show, comedian, Shearen Elebash; popular Ricky Skaggs; Vanessa Williams, the reigning Miss America; the Auburn University Singers; Pam Battles, then Miss Alabama; the University of Alabama Million-Dollar Band; Stephanie Ashmore, America's Junior Miss; and the Maxwell Air Force Base Band. An Atlanta singing group called "Mocha" brought down the house, and Bob Hope, whom I consider "Mr. America," held our patriotic Alabama citizens in the palm of his hand.

We were a hit! My part of the program—I opened with the National Anthem, and later sang an entertainment medley, accompanied by the University of Alabama Band, with my pianist Randy Cherry conducting the Maxwell Air University Band, closing with the "Battle Hymn of the Republic—went surprisingly well. But, best of all, everyone's hard work made the Performing Arts Centre of Selma and Dallas County become a reality. It's a great feeling to help bring a good thing into existence, our family agreed. Bobby, my thoughtful, studious son, who was home for the summer, like his sister Gloria, never became interested in show business, yet they helped me so I could commit to this show. The twins, on the other hand, worked like troupers. They have always enjoyed the excitement and chaos that go with any sort of entertainment production, though they've never been awed by the "glamour." They have seen how much hard work all that illusion requires.

During the days following "Stars Fell on Alabama," each of us opened up about "the business." Bill, our artist, discovered once again how much fun it is to work with sets, sound, and all sorts of other practical problems. The other kids remarked on how easily I had moved back into my old role. "Shouldn't you be praying about that, Mom?" Gloria asked pointedly.

"You shouldn't retire," Barbara said in that severe tone of voice that sounds exactly like me. "You have worked too hard to give it up so early."

Kids! What do they know? *Nevertheless,* I thought, *this stint has shown me something I could not have realized in any other way.* I had always supposed that singing was all I knew how to do. Silently I contemplated something amazing; my years of show-business experience had left me with a far broader knowledge than I ever dreamed I had. How ironic to realize that, just after I retired!

Memories of past work experiences continued to surface for the next several weeks. There was Lincoln Center, "A Salute to Congress," the ultimate in rehearsal, accompaniment, wardrobe, and acoustical glory. Then there were the many times I sang at the White House, always praying just before entering the state occasion, asking God to use my voice to minister to the President of the United States and his distinguished guests. On another unforgettable day, at solemn graveside services for President Lyndon Baines Johnson, via worldwide satellite, I sang the "Battle Hymn of the Republic" a capella, standing alone and facing the casket and a cold, bitter wind. I sang the same hymn at the Super Bowl in Miami in 1976. Then there were the occasions when I sang at both Democratic and Republican National conventions. Evangelist Billy Graham and I are the only persons who have appeared at both conventions.

God gave me a wonderful career, I thought. Now that it was over, I felt no regrets. There had been plenty of low spots, as well. I shuddered to recall some of the near catastrophes, and the times I had to improvise or fake it. Also, I recalled the many terrible, untuned pianos and ill-trained musicians my full-time conductor, Chuck Bird, had to battle.

The people who worked so hard to get me blacklisted never dreamed, in one sense, they were doing me a favor, I chuckled to myself. _Perhaps I'll accept an engagement here and there in the future, but no more ongoing jobs. Never!_

Each time we move beyond our personal battlefield or tragedy into a larger arena, we take a giant step toward survival. The Anita Bryant who moved to Selma to hide reminded me of the psalmist David, "a man after [God's] own heart" (1 Sam. 13:14), who fled from King Saul and hid in a cave.

But we can't hide forever. Little by little, Jesus helped instill in the kids and me new strengths and the will to survive. Somewhere, I got hold of the truth that we can't allow our emotions to drag us around by the nose. *I really wanted to live by faith—so easy to promise,* I thought, *and so impossible, in one's own strength, to do.* "I can do all things *through Christ*."

I found an article entitled "My Attitudes for Today." I do not know the author, but bless him or her for writing these truths:

Just for today:

I will try to live through this day only, and not set far-reaching goals to try to overcome all my problems at once. I know I can do something in twelve hours that would appall me if I felt that I had to keep it up for a lifetime.

I will try to be happy. Abraham Lincoln said, "Most folks are about as happy as they make up their minds to be." He was right.

I will not dwell on thoughts that depress me. I will chase them out of my mind and replace them with happy, joyful thoughts about the Lord.

I will adjust myself to what is. I will face reality. I will try to change those things I can change, and accept those things I cannot change.

I will try to improve my mind. I will not be a mental loafer. I will force myself to read something that requires effort (the Bible), thought, and concentration.

I will exercise my soul in three ways:

1. I will do a good deed for someone—without letting him know it. (If he or she finds out, it will not count.)

2. I will do at least two things that I know I should do, but have been putting off.

3. I will not show anyone that my feelings are hurt. They may be hurt, but for today I will not show it.

I will be agreeable and positive. I will look for the best side of everything and praise God for it, and I will not concern myself with the bad side of anything. I will look as well as I can, dress becomingly, talk softly, act courteously, and speak ill of no one. Just for today I'll try to improve no one except myself.

I will have a schedule or program. I may not follow it exactly, but I will have it, thereby saving myself from two pests: *hurry* and *indecision.*

I will have a quiet half hour with God. I will relax in Him. During this time I will reflect on my behavior and will try to get a better perspective of my life and its purpose.

I will be unafraid. I will gather the courage to do what is right, and I will take the responsibility for my own actions. I will expect nothing from the world, but I will realize that *as I give to the world, the world will give to me.*

As I moved out from my mental cave and into new positions in our new life, I wanted to "bloom where I was planted." God was teaching me that the way of personal survival comes through faith, hope, and love. I was working out my "salvation with fear and trembling" (see Phil. 2:12). When I needed answers, I found them in His Word: "I will guide thee with mine eyes" (Ps. 32:8). "Open thy mouth wide, and I will fill it" (Ps. 82:10). "I will never leave thee, nor forsake thee" (Heb. 13:5).

Even on days when I felt hopeless, I still sensed God's closeness. In my helplessness, He lifted me to my feet. And when I was dependent, I actually felt embraced by His everlasting arms. Gently, my Heavenly Father guided me into taking responsibility for things I never before had done. I founded a singles ministry—really just a one-on-one outreach to some hurting people. I also helped bring Val Balfour's original American version of the Oberammergau Passion Play to our community, although it turned out to be less than what we expected.

A step at a time, God led each of us forward. Bobby's turn came when he was accepted into Wheaton College in

Illinois. He felt elated. I tried not to show him that my heart was about to break. Since Bobby had spent his senior year in Miami, I had hoped he would spend more time in Selma with me, his brother, and sisters. Immediately after he left, I phoned a friend and poured out my grief.

"He had the worst time of all because of the divorce," I wept. "I ruined his senior year, maybe his life."

"Bobby seems unusually mature and well-adjusted," my friend remarked.

"You don't understand. I never took enough time to help him deal totally with the fact that he was adopted. He's a wonderful boy, and I haven't been the mother he deserves." I wept even harder.

"Enough, Anita!" my friend exclaimed. "I've heard you say you know you have one adopted child, but can't remember which one. There's nothing wrong with Bobby. He's fine. The problem is with you."

"I *know* that!" I told her, shocked at her lack of sympathy.

"Anita," she counseled me, "go ahead and have a good cry. You are a good mother and Bobby is a fine son, but he's the first to leave home and go away to college. It's the beginning of the empty-nest syndrome, and your emotions are normal. Go ahead and bawl, kid. We all do it."

Following my elder son's mature example, I took a good look at the next stage of my life. What was God's purpose for me? Where should I go, and what should I do? Was it time for me to move from Selma and enter some new training? *If only Gordona were here to help me think this through,* I thought.

This time, though, my circumstances had changed. Thanks to the Lord, and to numbers of His servants, I no longer leaned so often on the "arm of flesh."

Miraculously, I had somehow gained the confidence that I really could do all things through Christ. Daily, I felt Him strengthening me.

8
The Business of Business

I stepped off the stage at the Top Hat in Canada and walked into the audience, followed by the spotlight's dazzle. This fast-paced, upbeat show segment always was a favorite. Though I could not see past the bright lights, I loved the knowledge that my audience sat an arm's length away. Someone shoved something into my hand as I walked past a table. I didn't miss a beat, but glanced at what proved to be a snapshot of a man and woman, their two daughters, and myself.

Dick and Donalda Robards! I broke into a big smile and put a little extra "business" into the song. What a blessing.

We had decided that I must try to make a comeback. "We" means family and friends, plus hundreds of fans whose input arrived via mail and telephone. Meanwhile, the Lord brought several talented businessmen to offer me their time, expertise, and personal connections, simply because they believed I could and should return to my livlihood.

Certainly, the need was there. The two older kids were college-bound: Bobby to Wheaton, with Gloria the following year scheduled to enter Oral Roberts University in Tulsa. However, I longed to stay home with the twins until they graduated from high school. I thought I deserved that privilege.

My advisers, taking personal and professional factors

into consideration, hammered out a potentially feasible business strategy for me. The goal included several carefully selected projects—a TV special perhaps, convention bookings, a new book, record albums—at my own pace, and with a minimum of time away from home.

They also undertook to construct a plan wherein I could learn my own business and manage it myself. In the past, as I said, I attended to everything pertaining to the actual performance, while others handled the multitudinous details of travel, contracts, accounting, hiring backup musicians, secretarial work, and the rest. I had no time for the business part of the business. Though I earned large revenues, I had little idea of where the monies went, much less any real input into how they would be invested.

"I've been a fool," I said to the businessmen who had decided to help me form a corporation to bring my various enterprises under one legal umbrella.

"Not at all, Anita," one man responded. "Big success can become the greatest hazard of all. Few of us can oversee every aspect of our work. It's your job to learn how to guide your business, not do it all."

The day that discussion took place my friend was speaking to a woman who had just rushed home from driving kids to school, hastily cleaned the kitchen, then barely managed to slide into business clothing before the doorbell rang.

A corporation? *I have a hard enough time running a household,* I thought. My checkbook stayed in perpetual disarray; I needed to balance it before I dared pay any bills. *If I stay this much behind at home,* I asked myself, *how dare I think I can learn to manage a business?*

The question was not up for debate. Actually, I had no other acceptable options. As people continually pointed out, I was fortunate that my potential earnings far exceeded those of most housewives suddenly responsible for maintaining a household. That statement made me want to scream. As I tried to explain, I am not a negative person, but I do know the facts.

I had been blacklisted in my profession. I lacked both time and know-how to build the kind of organization adequate to handle sizable bookings. It takes big bucks to hire arrangers, musicians, sound and light technicians, and all the other needed expertise. Just thinking about those obstacles made me exhausted.

My attention immediately shifted from those objections, however, when I heard my attorney read the group's next suggestion. I should move to Atlanta. Atlanta? They had my full attention. Move again? I couldn't stand the thought. We had lived in Selma only three years.

Their reasoning made sense. My business requires, above all, travel. The drive from Selma to Birmingham or Montgomery, where I occasionally had bookings, took precious chunks of time and energy. The drive to Atlanta took even longer.

Atlanta, of course, is an international transportation hub. The city attracts important national and international conventions, which could be a natural source of work for me. I procrastinated for quite a while, but after much prayer ultimately made the decision.

Soon, our plans fell into place. I conceded that the move made perfect sense, but it was with a sad, hollow feeling that I contacted Nellie Shoults, a friend in real estate, and placed our home on the market. As before, the move took place during the summer while the kids visited their father.

"God, You have to help me," I prayed in utter desperation. Other than Charlotte Hale and Charlotte and Rankin Smith, with whom I usually stayed, I had contacted very few people in Atlanta who might help me settle there. Nevertheless, my plans were almost miraculously accomplished. In little more than *one week* I placed our home on the market, and with the help of another realtor friend, Peggy Yates in Atlanta, located and leased a townhouse,

My singing debut was at age two, singing "Jesus Loves Me" at First Baptist Church, Barnsdall, Oklahoma.

"In the Beginning"

Mom (Lenora), Dad (Warren), and me (Anita Jane) make three.

My dad, Warren Gene "Blackie" Bryant, quite a few years later in front of his ranch and garden

Guess I was about nine   Charlie Dry was ten.

Charlie and I in front of the old Dry homestead at 501 North
Mickle, Tishomingo, Oklahoma, where we played on their
old player piano

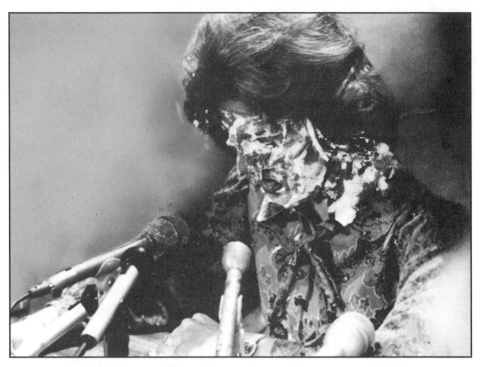

My features obscured by a banana cream pie, I cried in dismay. The pie thrower was a gay activist who approached me disguised as a reporter during a news conference in Des Moines, Iowa, October 1977.—AP/WIDE WORLD PHOTOS

Sharing my testimony in word and song in a local church—TOM WILLIAMSON

Bob Hope embraced me at a U.S.O. awards banquet, where he said, "This girl has brought more song, more joy, more hope, and more of good, old home to those boys in Vietnam, than anyone in the world, and I'll never forget her." Thanks, Bob!

Billy Graham was in Vietnam preaching to our troops. At my urging Bob Hope invited him to our Christmas show to say a prayer.

Press conference in New York City announcing "The Ellis Island Medal of Honor" recipients such as Cardinal Spellman and myself, along with many others

My daughter Barbara and I drinking Florida orange juice with Governor Bob Martinez at my induction into the Florida Citrus Hall of Fame as the first woman inductee

Getting acquainted: Front (left to right) Billy and Barbara and Stacy; Back (left to right) Bud and Gloria, Anita and Charlie, and Missy and Bobby—WENDELL CRITTENDEN

Charlie and I—it was a "Dry," but tearful, wedding (August 19, 1990).
—HOPE POWELL

"My Family—My Fortress" after the wedding: Front row, left to right: Hans-Walter (Bud) Sitarz (my son-in-law), Gloria Lynn Sitarz (my oldest daughter), Sam Page (my brother-in-law), Barbara Elisabet Green (my youngest daughter and twin to Billy), Sandra Jean Page (my sister), Anita and Charlie, Stacy Dry (Charlie's oldest daughter), Aniece Lenora Cate (Mama), George Richard (Paw Paw) Cate (my stepfather), William Bryant (Billy) Green (my youngest son); Back row, left to right: Robert E. Green, Jr. (my oldest son), Lisa Page (niece—now married to Randy Willard), Melissa (Missy) Green (daughter-in-law), Pat and Michelle Eitel (niece), and Kathy (niece) and Joey Odom—HOPE POWELL

Charlie's teaching me to be a real ranch hand—he even bought me "Okie" jeans and boots.—DAVID BELL PHOTOGRAPHY

This is serious stuff—probably concerns my budget!—DAVID BELL PHOTOGRAPHY

Before . . . Charlie said, "I'll build you a stage with a ramp."

After . . . with God's help he did it!—DAVID BELL PHOTOGRAPHY

"A Great First Season": Front row (Left to right) Jonathon O'Kain, keyboards, Wayne Campbell, conductor-pianist, Dexter Greene, drums, Bob Scrogham, guitar; Second row (l to r) Janet Galyen, Beegy Smith, Suzanne Long, Charlie Dry, Anita, Keith Wood, trumpet, Helaine Dowd, Marilyn Ray; Third row (l to r) Bette Steele, Wenona Ham; Fourth row (l to r) Wilma Howerton, Kirby Hoffman, bass guitar, Elizabeth Huff, Robin Sampley, Matt Merritt, Robert (Lance) Tolar—DAVID BELL PHOTOGRAPHY

Prayer time prior to every show with my friend and prayer partner, Charles Robertson, and members of my band (Wayne Campbell, right, pianist-conductor)

Taking time after the show to chat, sign autographs, and often pray with my audience—DAVID BELL PHOTOGRAPHY

What fun to go back to the Fifties!—DAVID BELL PHOTOGRAPHY

During the country-music medley I'm smiling, but my boots are killing me!—DAVID BELL PHOTOGRAPHY

"Welcome to the Anita Bryant Show in Eureka Springs, Arkansas." Call 501-253-5303.—DAVID BELL PHOTOGRAPHY

and moved many of our possessions into it. What's more, when the kids arrived at their new and still disorganized home, they instantly loved it. Never mind that hours earlier I had rushed out to buy new pillows, sheets, and other needed items.

A tiny feeling of self-satisfaction began to sneak up on me. Sure, I knew God did it: no human agent could have planned a move so wisely and directed it so smoothly. As Barbara would say, it was awesome! Still, I did handle all the details. I made decisions, phone calls, and headed off a few potential disasters. My self-respect moved up a notch or two. I needed that.

There was room in our compact townhouse for a tiny office, and our files and boxes of memorabilia could occupy a corner of the garage and the rest be stored. Thus we established the Beta Lambda Corporation's new headquarters, where we could begin to work in earnest.

The corporation's few investors agreed that my smartest move would be to hire an artist's manager to seek bookings and handle associated details. Ideally I would kibitz, so to speak, and learn everything he did. This would enable me to understand and eventually direct my own career, I reasoned. Also, it was understood that I would accept bookings I considered rewarding, and refuse those that did not interest me.

It took a considerable search to find Seth Marshall, a man who had gained an excellent, well-rounded show-business background in the competitive Los Angeles market, but also was an attorney. Recently divorced, Seth at that time was open to change, and he was willing to sign a year's contract and move to Atlanta. I ran into Julia Haar, a former Anita Bryant Singer (a group I formed in the early 70s) and hired her as my secretary. At the time my pianist-conductor, Lanier Motes, was of considerable help. I could see God's hand at work.

Burly young Seth, who reminded me of a big Teddy

bear with a genius brain, soon became part of our team. He updated my press kit and began to seek bookings. He found an apartment close by and set up his desk in a corner of my basement office, where I could hear telephone calls and conversations, but ignore them. Seth also began to make sense of my tangled household accounts and set up books for the business. _That was the greatest blessing of all,_ I thought. Seth never would pay the same bill twice, overlook an invoice, or lose important papers.

Just as I began to relax and congratulate myself on my greatly improved situation, it became apparent that Seth was bothered by something. He would drag upstairs for lunch, when we usually took time to coordinate our efforts, and I'd notice a frown on the babyish face beneath the reddish-brown beard.

"What's wrong, Seth?"

"Nothing. Just details. I'll handle them."

Soon, however, Seth was forced to level with me. He felt a mounting concern over the almost unanimous reluctance to hire Anita Bryant. Again and again, he heard the same excuses. They liked and admired me, thought my work was first class, knew that audiences loved my singing, but Anita Bryant was still too controversial. People were afraid to book me.

Now and again, Seth managed to wangle a contract, but despite his persistence, we obtained too few bookings. It scared us. When he did land a week-long engagement at the Top Hat in Windsor, Ontario, I at first refused it. Seth stood his ground.

"You've got to start somewhere, and this is it," he said.

"Seth, I don't do supper clubs."

"This club has an excellent reputation and hires the best entertainers. It won't damage you, and I feel certain it will help you. We need the revenue.

"Besides," came the final clincher as Seth herded me

into the proverbial corner, "you said you told God that you would go through any door He opened. He *must* have opened this door. I sure can't open them!"

Despite my deep dread concerning everything about that upcoming engagement, we went. As you know, our opening night audience totaled *fifteen,* the most humiliating evening in my career. Mike Drakitch, the club's owner, refused to break my contract. Magnificently, he decided to stick by me, even if it meant taking a financial loss.

The second night, the room held a respectable crowd, and they welcomed us with cheers, handwritten notes, and applause. That was the night when Dick and Donalda Robards appeared, and it was Dick who shoved the snapshot into my hand. That event galvanized every spiritual resource within me. It was as though God had sent angels into the restaurant, to provide me with instantaneous moral courage. My spirits skyrocketed at that moment, and from then on, our disaster turned to triumph.

Dick and Donalda Robards, Windsor citizens prominent in the real-estate profession, first met me in Miami Beach in 1977, at the height of my public controversy. Several weeks earlier, Dick had persisted until he managed to reach me by phone. He wanted me to testify at a prayer breakfast he planned to host at the Doral Country Club during an industry convention there.

"Frankly, I think my presence would jeopardize your breakfast, Mr. Robards," I told him. "I'll think about it and get back to you later."

Three weeks later, Dick phoned to tell me that he didn't care about any unpleasantness my presence in the hotel might engender. He felt that God had something for me to say to his prayer group. Reluctantly, I agreed.

Much later, I learned the rest of the story. When Dick approached his industry executives to request announcement space in the newsletter, they refused. Even my name was too controversial. Later, at the country club, Dick attempted to post signs directing guests to the room where I would speak. The hotel refused to allow him to post the signs or use my name.

"The only avenue I could follow," Dick told me later, "was that of word-of-mouth. I simply attended the Saturday night reception and told everybody I saw that Anita Bryant would sing and speak at our prayer breakfast. They were dumbfounded."

The next morning I slipped into a hotel room where 225 guests sat at tables for eight and awaited the woman who had become so notorious. God gave me a supernatural peace, yet I could not help noticing that the guests did not seem much like the typical Christian laypersons I usually met at affairs like this. "They really weren't," Dick later explained. "What happened was that Jews, Gentiles, Christians, and every other kind of person imaginable crowded into that prayer breakfast to hear what you had to say. Some were ready to grind you in a meat grinder."

Dick opened with prayer, then had others read from the New Testament and the Old Testament. He had no idea what I might say, but asked me to share the dramatic story of my twins' premature birth and near death, and my struggle to offer my babies' lives into the hands of Jesus Christ. That had been my first experience with relinquishment, and it still brings me to tears.

The program lasted two hours. I sang "How Great Thou Art" and "Praise the Lord, He Never Changes." At the end, those people gave me a standing ovation, but in my heart I accepted it for the Lord whose presence was very evident. According to Dick, at least one person at each table was openly weeping.

That morning in Miami Beach, at the height of a viciously ugly campaign to silence my voice and stamp out my livelihood, I saw Christian courage prevail. Dick and Donalda Robards had refused to be intimidated. Under God's leadership, Dick had gone steadily forward, and God's plan prevailed. Even though my knowledge of Dick and Donalda was limited, God meant for us to meet.

That Sunday morning in Miami Beach, I had no idea that I'd ever see them again, but would always remember Dick's godly example of quiet bravery against strong opposition. Because of him, I felt fresh courage.

So, seven years later, Dick Robards drove home from his office in Windsor, Ontario, and happened to pass the Top Hat Supper Club. _Anita Bryant!_ "I felt thunderstruck to see your name on the marquee," he later told me. "We had plans we could not break that Monday night, but made sure we got tickets for Tuesday."

What a difference a day made. Once again, God sent Christians to put steel into my spine. Not only did Dick and Donalda show up, with some of their seven fine children, but they spread the word. Soon Christian people from Canada and nearby Detroit flocked to support me. Mike Drakitch appeared gratified and mystified. When I showed him some of the little notes his customers passed to me, it was like God's testimony to both of us. "Hi, Anita. We praise God you are working again. We have been praying for your return." Or, "God bless you, Anita. Thank you for taking a public stand for Him." I read each precious message with tears in my eyes.

Besides attending the show several times that week, Dick and Donalda invited me to visit their home. We had a time of renewal there—sharing, prayer, and browsing through family albums filled with mementoes of one Christian family's milestones and successes. We laughed, relaxed, and nibbled delicious tea cakes like those Grandma Berry used to make.

I was to meet this dynamic couple later, at the 1990 Presidential Prayer Breakfast in Washington, D.C.— another meaningful occasion.

Our nation was planning tremendous celebrations and commemorations for the soon-to-be restored Statue of Liberty and Ellis Island, and I longed to take part. That was not business, of course, but a deeply sentimental, personal desire to involve myself in honoring those cherished national symbols.

Atlanta had been chosen to mount a major Southeastern funding campaign for the project. Lee Iacocca, the Chrysler Corporation CEO whose parents emigrated from Italy and became naturalized Americans, led the gigantic efforts. *What if I telephoned Mr. Iacocca and offered my services?* I wondered. Then I thought, *if my name still is too controversial and he turns me down* . . .

I had to stop such thoughts. While it was true that I never expected where my next slap would come from, I absolutely *could not* allow myself to live in fear of personal attack. I made up my mind to contact Mr. Iacocca. Reminding myself that I probably had received more medals and commendations from patriotic organizations and branches of the U.S. armed services than almost any other American woman, I decided I would stand on my record and assume the best. I suppose that old Indian stubborn streak (I am almost a fourth part Native American) helped.

It took several telephone efforts to reach Mr. Iacocca but eventually we connected. "Are you *the* Anita Bryant?" someone always asked, and by now that question almost gave me giggles. I felt like telling them if I were *another* Anita Bryant, I'd think seriously about changing my name!

Mr. Iacocca did not spurn my offer at all, but sounded very nice. I told him I was struggling to make a professional comeback, that his book, which described the enormous career obstacles he overcame, gave me hope. He responded quietly, almost humbly. "Keep trying, Anita. Remember, if I can make a comeback, anybody can."

Working on behalf of "The Lady," Miss Liberty, took my mind off my own struggles and heightened my spirits. I was named chairman of the Southeast area's Ladies for Liberty, a committee of public-spirited women who lent not only their names, but their considerable powers, to the cause. The campaign took time I really couldn't spare, but we persevered. "I assumed you would be chairman in name only," J. Edward Easler II of the Atlanta headquarters told me. "I would not lend my name if I were not willing to work," I assured him.

"Meanwhile, back at the ranch," my staff firmed up plans for me to tape, as a celebrity reporter, some interviews for a local television series on station WAGA-TV. "Not a blockbuster contract," I remarked, "but praise God anyhow. Maybe this is another of His doors."

The first show we filmed went well, according to the producers. The second would be taped following a quick trip to New York, where I was scheduled to make a network television appearance, have wardrobe fittings, and a photo session at the Statue of Liberty site.

New York offered us an unseasonably bleak and windy day for May, not at all the sort of weather you'd choose for photo purposes. I shivered in the old fur coat I had dug out at the last moment, and the wind and raw air played havoc with my voice and my hairdo. I longed to finish the shoot and return to Manhattan for hot coffee at some cozy deli.

A tremendous awe sweeps over you when you stand at the foot of the immense statue which guards the New York harbor and proclaims liberty, under God, to all the world. Once I had been pictured against that majestic background for a record jacket which covered my album of patriotic hymns, anthems, and songs. *Now,* I thought, *everything about me—and even about the great Statue of Liberty—seemed to have changed.* Up close, you could see that nearly a century's exposure to salt, air pollution, and acid rain had caused the copper structure to crumble. The marvelous Lady looked so fragile. . . .

A workshop set up at the statue's base teemed with men so busy they did not raise their heads to notice we were there. "Some of the world's most famous craftsmen are here," Ted Easler explained. "They came from France and are some of Europe's most highly specialized copper-smiths. They are rebuilding the statue France gave to the United States of America in 1886."

We finished the photography and awaited arrival of the ferry boat which would return us to Manhattan. As I shivered in the wind, a thought occurred to me. "Ted, several years ago, a man who works here wrote me a moving letter and sent me a light bulb which had been used in the statue's torch. I don't remember the man's name, but do you suppose we could find him?"

At the main office, our query received an immediate response. "That would be Charlie DeLeo," they told us. "We'll send him to meet you."

Mr. DeLeo, a dark-haired working man with tar on his hands, had been repairing a roof. He approached me nervously, looking both shy and amazed. "Miss Bryant? You wanted to see me?" When I asked him about the gigantic light bulb taken from the torch held by the hand extended from Miss Liberty's thirty-six-hundred-pound arm, his poise returned and he talked freely.

"I remember you from overseas, when you sang to us servicemen," he explained. "After I was discharged I came straight to the Statue of Liberty and asked for a job. I believe I'm supposed to work here. Sometimes I take my lunch and climb high up into the statue, look out over New York City and the Atlantic Ocean, and pray for America.

"When you were under attack, Miss Bryant, I'd go up into the torch and pray for you. It wasn't fair, the way you were persecuted. I want you to know that I prayed for you every day."

Charlie DeLeo's words left me speechless. I stood there, tears filling my eyes, thinking he surely didn't look like an angel, dressed in his khaki pants and dark windbreaker, but as certain as I ever was certain of anything . . . his words came directly from God to me. That miserably cold day, all my fatigue and anxiety and everything of this world were swept away by the wind of God's Holy Spirit. That moment He transformed and energized me, and placed profound awe and peace into my soul. As I took Charlie DeLeo's hand and then hugged him, thanking him as best I could, I felt I was standing on holy ground.

The short, unremarkable ferry ride to New York seemed bathed in new light. The wind still whistled around the boat, but I felt an indescribable warmth and joy. Throughout the rest of the day, tears came to my eyes whenever I thought of God's goodness to me at the foot of that magnificent landmark, the Statue of Liberty.

I got my wish. Our driver knew the best deli in Manhattan and promptly delivered us there. With my thoughts fixed on a plump Reuben sandwich and some hot coffee, yet still pondering the amazing events of the hour before, it's no wonder that I hardly noticed our surroundings, or that the proprietor stopped everything and rushed towards us. "Anita Bryant!" he shouted, alerting everyone in the crowded place. "God bless you! Thank you for the stand you took, and welcome to our city!"

As we proceeded to our table, other diners greeted me with equal warmth. I felt tremendously astonished, moved, and elated at the unexpected attention. I had become so accustomed to the reverse.

Back home in Atlanta that night, tired but joyously confident, I dumped my suitcases in the bedroom and started hanging clothes in the closet. The telephone rang.

"I wanted to reach you before the press does," my business advisor said. "I'm sorry, but you have been fired from WAGA-TV. The story hits the press tomorrow."

"Fired? Why on earth . . ."

"There have been protests from homosexual viewers about your part of the show, so they decided to cancel. They claim you are too controversial."

"How can they do that? You mean I really am not supposed to make a living? How can I provide for my children?''

"Don't worry, Anita, I'm on my way to Atlanta. We'll take care of this problem tomorrow. We'll come up with a statement to the press. I just didn't want you caught unprepared in case the press starts calling you tonight."

I felt totally crushed, and I wept. Something told me we couldn't just "take care of the problem" tomorrow, that it would follow me everywhere, that I couldn't escape it. The more I considered my circumstances, the more drained and despairing I felt. I wanted to leave Atlanta, run away and hide. Finally, too weary for words, I crawled into bed, knowing that first thing tomorrow, I must face the lions.

After a session of fitful prayer and before falling to sleep, I was reminded by the Lord just what I had received earlier that day. I thought of the dark-haired workman who took his brown bag lunch into the very torch of the Statue of Liberty and prayed for me. Charles DeLeo's job called for him to clean and service the torch, shining the two-hundred panes of glass and replacing burned-out bulbs. He had made that torch into a chapel where he kept rosary beads, religious articles, and the Bible, and prayed each day.

God would not leave me comfortless. I slept well and awoke fit and well-equipped to meet with my business advisors and hash out a statement to the press. The conference proved lively, the sort of situation I once had dreaded—but something had happened in my spirit during the past twenty-four hours. No more would I live by fear, I decided. I would face my adversaries not in anger or bitterness, but in love, conciliation, and God's truth. That always had been my stance, though I had been misquoted and misrepresented time and time again. I would not allow hopelessness or fear to make me depart from it.

Though I recall few of the media's questions or my answers, the bottom line was this: "If there's no room in this country for an Anita Bryant, then this is no longer America."

The television station's decision to fire me created public debate for weeks. I received stacks of mail, nearly all of it supportive. Christian attorneys offered to represent me free should I choose to sue the station. Even the ultraliberal American Civil Liberties Union sided with me and offered legal help. My advisors believed I had an airtight case against the station and should seize my legal advantage, but I refused. "I can't endure any more media bombardment and lies about my stand nor can my children," I told them. "I don't want to spend weeks in court, and I don't believe God wants me to take any more time out of my life for this kind of chaos. I just want to work and provide for my children."

Those were the public and tumultuous conditions under which I tried to conduct business. At times the hope of success seemed preposterous. I saw that my notoriety and the controversy surrounding my name would mean a steep career climb, many slips, and much hard work to find even the tiniest toehold. *Like the Statue of Liberty,* I thought, *perhaps my life had eroded so dangerously. . . .*

My heart and spirit rejected that thought. I remembered the coppersmiths working so diligently to strengthen and restore each inch of that magnificent Lady. Just so, I believed, God had planned a far more incredible restoration for me, His battered and broken child. In my mind I really had two choices. I could either give in and give up or get up and get out of my destructive circumstances.

That image of the Statue of Liberty restoration helped me "set my face like a flint," to use a biblical phrase meaning sheer determination. I would build my business, would exercise the gifts God gave me, and would support my children.

How? I did not know. I did know, however, that despite all obstacles, with God's help, I could do it.

9
Money and Prosperity

s I tried to straighten out my finances, my mind rolled back to our Selma days. "First, you need to make a budget," my friend Gordona Duca advised.

"OK, what then?"

"We'll take it from there. Your household budget is your starting place."

To a highly successful businesswoman like Gordona, my financial questions obviously seemed far less complex than I thought they were. Because our home in Miami Beach still had not sold, I lacked available funds to apply to our then-current home in Selma. That problem required financial decisions I felt inadequate to make. As it turned out, Gordona helped me find ways to bridge the gap.

That accomplished, Gordona seemed to think a household budget would be my next step. "We'll look it over, and I'll help you see exactly where you stand," she encouraged. "Send it to me when you're ready."

I couldn't imagine when that might be. Although Gordona called from Tulsa frequently and inquired about my budget two or three times, I put her off. Those things take time, I said, and we were still unpacking. I'd get to it soon.

Then came a trip back home to Tulsa, where I met with Russell McCraw, a most interesting Christian brother with whom I developed an immediate friendship. Russell, too, could offer sound help with my financial questions. Well schooled and experienced in finance, he was not at all fazed by my hopeless quandary. "I agree, a budget is the right place to start," he said, speaking as kindly and tactfully as you would to a teenager.

Desperately, I took the plunge. Obviously, it was time to tell the truth.

"Russell," I gulped, "what *is* a budget?"

So began the education of Miss Anita, in a subject I dreaded and had skillfully avoided during my entire adult life—money. The topic, though vitally necessary, was thoroughly distasteful to me. I suppose I had the notion that I should continue to work insanely hard year after year, receiving more money than I knew what to do with, with never any accounting required from me. After all, what are accountants for?

Truthfully, I was not arrogant about the subject, merely ignorant and scared. I was used to having nothing but the best, and now here I was with very little money and some large spending habits. As my friend Teddy Heard would have said, I had a big ego hole where my financial know-how should have been. Now we had arrived at the place where I could no longer fake it. I had to get some basic financial education and had to do it right away. Our available funds were streaming out at an alarming rate, with precious few monies trickling in.

Russell took on the task of helping me draw up a household budget. He showed me how to list my basic monthly expenses, estimate such options as travel, personal items, and other extras, and to prorate sums for clothing, tuition, and the like. It wasn't easy, especially with me arguing about much of his advice, but Russell persisted until he could present me with a set of neat, clearly itemized sheets. I felt proud of our success. *My budget looked terribly professional,* I thought.

"Huh, this looks like a municipal budget," Gordona

wisecracked, as she glanced through the pages. "What's this twenty-five dollars a week for McDonald's?"

"Well, the kids like burgers and pizza a couple of times a week, and I thought . . ."

Gordona's laugh stopped me. "You've made a good beginning," she said. "You can refine this as you go."

Actually, I was not into refining our finances. What I lacked—and it was a huge lack—was basic financial knowledge. Like many other women and some men in high-income brackets, I kept myself aloof from every financial consideration. I paid the drugstore or hairdresser or my church offerings by writing a personal check, but those checks really didn't have to balance, according to me. And when our New York accountants had come to Miami to consult us about taxes, investments, and various other expenditures, I made it my business to be elsewhere.

The only time I had any significant input into deciding where our money would be spent was when years ago I had become convinced that we should tithe.

"Off the top? Gross income?" My husband was at first aghast. He had tried hard to make me understand that in our tax bracket, we had to earn two dollars for each dollar we spent. "Do you know how many actual dollars you are talking about?"

I didn't, but I stood my ground. According to the way I understood Scripture, your tithe is one tenth of all you earn or receive. *Not* after taxes, expenses, or anything else, but the "firstfruits" of your labors. I believed that was what God wants and expects, and I wanted with all my heart to obey Him.

Phil, our accountant, kept silent while we discussed the matter. When we at last asked Phil's opinion, our friend, whose clientele were mostly entertainers, said, quietly, "Those of my clients who give God their first 10 percent never seem to suffer any monetary problems."

So it was settled. We tithed. We prospered. But that was then, before the collapse of my career and the divorce. Should I still tithe, with my circumstances so volatile and reduced? Would God expect me to give Him my first 10 percent, or should I first pay bills and provide for my household?

Scripture provides the answer, of course. The first tenth a believer earns is not "mine," but His. I knew in my heart that God would provide for us, no matter what might come. It was from love, not duty, that I decided I must continue to tithe, although I admit I felt a tinge of apprehension about it. That decision, however, was to set me free.

Then came some tough times. The houses in which I had tied up our money took forever to sell. The Miami house, a large estate, had been placed on the market during a bad real-estate sales season. The Selma house needed a few structural changes, I thought, and those had proved expensive. After we moved to Atlanta I rented at first. Then Gloria finished college and moved back with me and the twins, so I later bought still another house, contingent on selling the one in Selma, and again, the real-estate market remained incredibly flat.

By now, I desperately needed to find how to produce some financial sleight of hand, but had little expertise. My real-estate holdings had been leveraged to the hilt. I worried constantly, and often looked at my bills and cried. I was in one of those depressions the day Billy wandered in and asked, "Where is your faith? Don't you have faith as a grain of mustard seed, Mom?"

I did. The faith was there, all right, but like many another Christian, I needed to learn that faith is not all that God expects of us. He also expects us to gather our physical, mental, and spiritual resources and put them to use. He expects us to make wise decisions. He wants to guide us in every detail of our lives.

But I felt so stupid. I hated to keep asking such dumb

questions about stuff everybody else seemed to understand. Whenever it came to the subject of money, my self-esteem would plummet, and you'd have to wipe me up off the basement floor. Financial discussions usually left me feeling uncomfortable, embarrassed, and exhausted.

My list of rash, ill-advised, or just plain unfortunate money moves would fill a book. They might have continued to this day, except that I enrolled in a Christian financial seminar and began to study God's instructions about money, and the means of utilizing the wealth God gives us.

Had I attended that seminar straight off, the episode at the Miami Beach savings-and-loan institution would not have happened. Prior to leaving Florida, when the divorce was announced, I walked in one day to open a checking account, and the person I approached looked at me as if I were out of line. "Ma'am, you need a bank. This is a savings-and-loan institution, but there's a bank down the street."

What's the difference? I asked myself. They both looked alike. I felt mortified by my goof, however, and was sure everybody must have laughed the moment I left. I was wearing large sunglasses and prayed no one recognized me. I was humiliated.

Today, I would recommend that every man, woman, and certainly every head of a household should attend a Christian financial seminar. If you know nothing whatever about money, that's your starting place. And if you are financially astute, you can learn still more of God's principles.

For example, many people are amazed to learn that the Bible contains more teachings about money than all other subjects except one—that of salvation. Jesus often preached about money. The Bible tells us again and again that God desires us to prosper, although His idea of prosperity extends far beyond material wealth.

Those who study the Bible for ways to enrich life—not

only mentally and spiritually, but financially as well—discover some eye-openers. You learn that giving is central to all prosperity. You begin to understand that God has not designed us for lives of want, stress, financial pressures, greed, or desperation, but He yearns to guide us into skillful choices which produce a balanced life, free from any kind of excess.

Such lessons are not learned overnight, and for me it will continue as a lifelong lesson. Although some people seem naturally talented at using money wisely and creatively, others must learn to adopt a new mind-set. We have to learn to pray for specific guidance before making business or personal decisions. Not only do we learn to place our needs on His altar, but our desires as well. Then we put aside our pride and allow Him to work.

I had to pray for God to show me why the subject of money aroused such terrible fear and anxiety within me. Had my humble, sometimes materially deprived childhood played a part? Then, after achieving professional success, why had I always struggled against extravagance? God showed me, though, that mainly I feared I might not be adequate to take care of my children. His answer? To remind me daily that these are His children; I gave each of my four young people to God early in their lives.

God takes care of His children. He would provide for Bobby, Gloria, Billy, Barbara, and Anita, too. Those ponderings in my heart brought me to know Jehovah Jireh, the biblical name for our Father which means "God Will Provide." I was acquainted with that name and what it means, yet did not truly know the providing love of our Heavenly Father, whose divine provision never ceases.

Gradually, as I took our needs to Him in the privacy of my prayer closet, His hands opened and filled our every necessity. Sometimes, hours before a payment was due, I had to force myself to believe, to stand on God's promises, and hold onto what He told me. Always our needs were met through some unexpected means—repayment of an almost forgotten loan, perhaps, or a royalty check from albums recorded years ago, from a recording company that no longer chose to sponsor me, and sometimes through family or friends, who gave outright, knowing our needs.

One of the most important steps toward prosperity that God showed me was that of self-forgiveness. As a major earner, I had been trusting but not wise. When God gives you money-making abilities, He holds you accountable. You are His steward. I saw that I had shifted that responsibility to others, refusing to grow into the knowledge of how God would have me utilize the monies I had received. Though I truly had tried to put Jesus first, in this area I had been blind. I was full of fear, not faith. I needed to repent of those mistakes and forgive myself for making them.

On occasion, I took money from my tithe to help a needy person. My tithe account was set up in a special checking account, so I always placed a note in my desk— I.O.U., God—until the money could be returned for tithing purposes.

That special tithe account represented 10 or 15 percent of my business account, and I took pleasure in following its progress. I recalled that my part-time secretaries always kept records, and I learned to follow their examples. Those first much-erased accounting sheets represented, for me, all kinds of stubborn plugging away at what literally felt like a foreign language. I hated it but made myself do it.

Gordona Duca had her attorney show me how to prepare a financial statement, and her CPA helped me with my tax returns. Those gentlemen had to explain finances to me as simply as you would to a child.

The lessons derived from learning how to use money go far beyond mere money, of course. Our money, actually, becomes the means whereby God teaches about true prosperity. For example, when I refused to allow myself to lust after the "perfect" dress, God gave me another like it, yet a better style, for half of what I might have paid.

Driving our beat-up van around Selma was more fun than driving my imported sports car had been, and it evidenced the down-to-earth, laid-back personal life-style we enjoyed. Also, when I wrecked the van, I didn't mourn the damage, but thanked God for delivering *me* unharmed!

I began to understand how the proper use of money leads to proper perspectives, as we learn how to live according to God's values. Probably I'll never outgrow my delight in beautiful clothes, but because of my business, I owned wonderful fashions in abundance. What I soon realized, though, is that I must keep my body under subjection. Even five unwanted pounds meant some of my loveliest items would have to hang in the closet unworn, with no budget for larger-size replacements.

By insisting that I stay in shape, and making myself exercise, I can still use costumes in my act that have lasted twenty years. Those are expensive items, and I thank God for them.

Those few small examples illustrate the attitude changes God longs to make in some of us materialistic Americans. You wake up one morning fretting, turn to God with the problem, then realize how far He has led you from where you used to be. You think about your friends and all their generous help and advice.

I learned that bankers are not heartless. Even some bank executives I did not know took chances on me simply because they admired and respected me, and wanted to help. God sent each of these men and women into my life as my needs appeared. Many times they provided an outlet for my family to continue unharmed, when there seemed no way out of a particular financial dilemma.

We must do our part, also. Like many other people, I find credit cards a trap. It's too easy to overspend, and I still blow it at times. Some women, in particular, find it easy to rationalize unwise spending. It can be tempting to use a credit card to charge against an expected check. Sometimes that check is *not* in the mail.

During my show-business years I never shopped sales. Now I shop wisely and wait for sales. Fashion magazines and upscale catalogs don't make me discontented these days, either. I simply tear out the pages with pictures of desirable items and keep them in a stack. After a while, you're not so gung ho about things you thought you wanted.

As I made myself learn how to balance my checkbooks, keep accurate financial records, compile receipts for tax purposes, and the like, I began to feel the old terrors about money management slip away. With four young people to see through college, I learned to do some high-powered juggling at times, but it turned out OK. All our needs were met. God is still meeting our needs.

Sometimes, though, I admit I wondered if God would let us sink down to a zero bank balance. If so, how would I handle that? When it happened, I discovered that being broke, and being aware you have done all you can, sometimes provokes a feeling of freedom that comes when, having done all, you stand. When you are sure the Lord wants you to give away that last ten-dollar bill in your pocketbook you silently argue with Him for a moment or two, then relinquish the money.

Are You serious, Lord? you think. *We need milk. I have no more money for groceries.*

Then you return home, having almost forgotten you gave your last money away, and find an unexpected check in the mail—a refund from the power company or another unexpected source. You laugh at the check, knowing that God knew it was there all the time, just as all of His provisions always are.

So we learn. Jehovah-jireh, my divine Provider, reached out to us one year when I could see no work or income in sight, and provided a job I had not even prayed to get. The Reverend Fletcher Brothers, who heads Freedom Village in Lakemont New York, remembered my ministry to children and contacted me to serve as spokesperson for his nationally known ministry to hurting and abused teenagers, including alcohol and drug addicts, prostitutes, and those with incorrigible behavior problems.

For more than a year, God used me in the Freedom Village ministry, thereby providing a regular salary which proved to be the only income we had at that time. This provision arrived "out of the blue," after a diligent search for me on the part of Pastor Brothers, who did not have my new address.

Totally dependent on God at that point, I had no way to foresee that He could and would link me with a ministry so important, and so close to my heart. I bless Pastor Brothers for inviting me to share his marvelously important and successful work. God then opened up an opportunity for me to represent *The Rainbow Study Bible* published in El Reno, Oklahoma.

As the kids and I learned more about trusting God and as we tithed through thick and thin—cut out frills, enjoyed all He gave us, and became better problem solvers—real prosperity emerged.

Our sense of gratitude flourished. Every holiday dinner, new dress, used car, tuition check, job offer—everything that makes up life—came from God, and we acknowledged it. We treasured our family milestones, too, all the big and little events, and so much more.

Prosperity means that we realize and fully understand that "Every good gift and every perfect gift . . . cometh from the Father" (Jas. 1:17). Whether we are abased, as the apostle Paul said, or whether we abound, we learned to be happy. Now, that's real wealth!

10
By the Grace of God

ritish evangelist Oswald Chambers described grace as "the overflowing favour of God," and said you can "always reckon it is there to draw upon." For years I have used *My Utmost for His Highest,* a book of daily devotions from Chambers's teachings, and each day's message seems to strike at the heart of that moment's need in my life.

Somehow, though, I missed part of his central message. First, we come into God's salvation only through our own desperate need and absolute poverty of spirit; and second, our own talents and self-sufficiency often hinder God's grace in our lives. Through our destitution, Chambers wrote, we come to God in the first place, then see His awesome work in us through the daily workings of our lives.

After moving to Atlanta, I wasn't thinking about such fundamentals the afternoon I entered Jack McDowell's Atlanta office. Jack had agreed to advise me about some business matters. As usual, I needed solutions *now.* Tall, dynamic, and soft-spoken, Jack McDowell is the sort of Christian business leader whose name stands for the highest personal and professional principles and conduct. He had centered his life's work around the Salvation Army's outreach and objectives, and his colleagues call him "the officer without a uniform."

Peggy, Jack's beautiful Austrian-born wife, is known as

Peggy Weber Francis of the candle-making family whose artistry dates back to 1512 in Vienna. When Peggy expanded her family's business into America following World War II, Jack helped guide her into the phenomenal success she enjoys. I was assured Peggy and Jack liked me and believed in me, and felt willing to share advice and encouragement.

That day I poured out my perplexities on an attentive and sympathetic Jack, hoping he could help me. It seemed I had reached an impasse, but maybe Jack's incisive grasp of facts might produce a new approach to my problems.

"Anita, sometimes it's a real blessing to reach the place where everything seems blocked no matter which way you turn," Jack said. His voice sounded vibrant and enthusiastic, as though he were congratulating me for being smart enough to have entered a dead-end street, but I began to relax.

"Your answers are there, OK," he continued, "but you are looking in the wrong place."

"Jack, I pray without ceasing."

"Goes without saying," he replied. "I know you go to God first. But you still don't see answers, and you wonder why He hasn't shown you what to do next. I think I have an insight about that."

"Please tell me!"

"Anita, it's exciting. You are . . . how old?" I told him. "OK, you have that many years' experience. Everything God ever gave you is walking around today in your shoes. He has given you a lifetime of specific experiences and knowledge. Those cumulative experiences are stored in your mind, body, and spirit, waiting for you to tap into them. Those are God's gifts to you."

My heart sank, and a lump formed in my throat. I was in a personal crisis, and Jack spoke to me about gifts. I had been taking career steps, OK, but my heart was not in it. The more I moved towards career, the more that neglected woman—my basic self—cried for attention. Now this man was talking to me about using my gifts. *But what about* me? I cried out silently. *Does anyone care about the real* me? *I am so tired of forever serving a talent and hearing people talk about my responsibilities to my* career. *What about my very* life?

"You can find every answer you need for your life because the answers are there, waiting for you to claim them," Jack continued. "Jesus said, 'The kingdom of God is within you.'"

"But how? Exactly how do I claim my answers?" I asked, almost exasperated. It seemed as though Jack had not heard a single fact I told him. Was he going to offer me nothing but platitudes and generalities? I felt intense disappointment.

"I am about to tell you how. This may sound simplistic, but it will work. I want you to go home and begin to list every good gift God has given you. Everything. List dozens and dozens of gifts that are especially yours. This exercise may take days, but make your list as complete as possible, praying as you explore your life and yourself.

"Anita, it is from your life and the gifts God gave you that you will find specific answers to your needs. It works every time."

Part of me understood Jack's words and recognized the truth in them, but part of me felt as though I were suffocating. Tears came to my eyes as I asked, "Are you saying that God requires me to return to the stage and sing? Jack, there are no songs left. I'm trying, but my heart's not in it.

"I know God gave me a talent," I wept, "and I developed it to the best of my abilities. I have worked hard all my life, even as a child. But is this all there is? Why do other women get to stay home and rear their children? What's wrong with wanting to be married, keep house, and just stay home?"

Jack stood his ground. "Nothing at all," he answered with quiet intensity. "That's the whole point of what I am saying. When you list *each* of your gifts, you discover the breadth of your personality traits and talents. You learn that answers for your life can come from several angles, not just one.

"This kind of scrutiny helps you stave off burnout and maximize your life. Obviously you must work, but God considers *you*, Anita Bryant, to be the apple of His eye. You are to offer yourself, your work, and everything you have to Him, so you can glorify Him through every facet of your life.

"You and Peggy are so alike," Jack smiled. "So talented, intense, and focused. You give everything you have to each job you take on, then wonder why you feel wiped out. It is hard to learn to balance our lives—work and personal growth, spiritual and intellectual growth, the love each of us needs—but that is what you are doing now.

"List your gifts carefully and fully, then offer them back to God. He will help you build your life into something glorious. Remember, God never compels us to exercise our talents to the destruction of our other gifts," Jack reassured me. "He is not like that.

"You will find wonderful answers, if you try. Remember, Peggy and I love you. Please let us know what our Lord Jesus Christ shows you!"

Jack's advice did sound simplistic, I mused, *but it also felt right*. Driving down Roswell Road in the Atlanta area toward home at rush hour, I felt my spirits begin to lift. I felt peace. Nobody else I knew would have told me what Jack McDowell had said, and certainly he offered no pat answers, but I felt a familiar sense of excitement building. I would do what Jack had suggested. *Then,* I wondered, *what will God show me next?*

There's all the difference in the world between seeking God with confidence and seeking Him in panic. When I propped up on my big bed with pencils and a large pad of paper to begin Jack McDowell's assignment, a resurgent thrill and feelings of excitement and adventure rose within me. This would be interesting.

Thirty minutes later it didn't seem so easy. I had written a dozen obvious "gifts" on the big sheet of paper, then had run out of ideas. I could recall plenty of negatives about Anita Jane Bryant, but honestly couldn't find many positives. My excitement began to ebb, and I picked up the telephone and called a close friend.

"Help me with this," I asked, feeling foolish.

"You didn't say 'intelligent,'" she pointed out.

"I'm stupid. Why else is my life such a mess?"

"You didn't say 'good mother' either," she commented.

"A good mother wouldn't be divorced and desperately trying to provide for her kids, and failing," I came back.

"You are supposed to list all your *gifts* from God, Anita, not sit there judging yourself. Be objective. Start being honest," she admonished, and began to enumerate. "You are intelligent. You are a good mother. You have wonderful children. You possess a lot of physical energy. You know many people all over the United States . . ."

"Most of them hate me," I interjected.

"You repent of that! This is an assignment, not a pity party. Get with it. I want to see at least one hundred gifts on that list by tomorrow!"

Why do I dwell on this episode? Because Jack Mc-Dowell was right, and the girl friends who helped me with his suggestion were right. The gifts are there; they exist; they can be listed. Once listed, as Jack well comprehended, you see with your eyes that God will never leave you or forsake you. You realize that He has been with you always, He is with you today, and He has given you everything you need to handle life. Besides, if you can't love who you are, how can you love your neighbor as yourself? (God's Commandment) So, receive the Lord's gift— *you!*

As we compiled individual lists of gifts and traits, my friends and I wrote down some funny items. Good at tennis? Wrapping gifts? Dimples? Straight teeth? Sense of humor?

It really was fun, and profitable. I don't remember how my predicaments worked out, but I shall always remember Jack's advice to me. He reminded me once again of God's unfailing grace toward Anita Bryant, or toward anyone who is willing to receive it.

At that time, one friend pointed out that during my travails I learned I really could deal with media people. I howled at that, but she insisted. "You interview well. You think things through more carefully . . . don't speak so impulsively . . . aren't terrified anymore."

If that was almost right, I reflected, *it probably began in Selma, Alabama.* Would you believe God let me buy a house there next door to the local newspaper editor? Shelton and Ann Prince, our neighbors, were newspaper folks to the core. Shelton and I weren't always agreeable on certain issues, but as we learned more about each other it amazed us how much we could agree on. I soon discovered that his staff writer Jean Martin, like other local news people I encountered, dedicated herself to fair and accurate reporting.

Nevertheless, I still felt wary of and even hostile to the media. During the months when my kids played with the Prince kids and we adults enjoyed cookouts and occasional parties, Ann and Shelton became dear friends as well as neighbors. Ann also worked with me on the Performing Arts Board. Gradually I was able to make Ann understand that I had endured some truly vicious media distortions and lies, to the point I felt it would be impossible for me ever to trust media people again. The press has tremendous power to influence public opinion and to harm the reputation of an individual, I pointed out.

Ann Prince agreed but reminded me that freedom of the press represents one of America's greatest strengths. Though there may be bad members of this or any other institution, we should not condemn the entire profession.

Good people like Ann and Shelton Prince helped me change some of my attitudes.

Later in Atlanta, where I dreaded receiving media attention, I recall an interview with a young woman writer who confided that her father was near death. We stopped our interview, joined hands and prayed together, not as interviewer and interviewee, but as two Christian daughters who loved their fathers. Each of us felt God's grace within that workaday situation.

Still later, most of the news media took my side when a television station in Atlanta fired me for being "controversial." Whether or not the media liked me, most stood up for my rights on this particular issue. Shelton also wrote an editorial in support of me. By the grace of God, my terrible media wounds began to heal.

At intervals, unforgettable personal miracles transpired when God led one or another of His servants to intercede for me in some amazing way. Evangelist James Robison stands out in my memory. A dynamic, Bible-preaching man who never would compromise the gospel, James, I figured, like most other high-profile Christian ministers, would have nothing more to do with me after my divorce.

I should not have judged him. It happened that James Robison knew the particulars of my divorce situation, but he showed love and compassion and affirmed me as a person, but stated he still hated divorce. He made many phone calls in my behalf and wrote letters to a number of prominent pastors in which he vouched for me and supported me. Because James was willing to say, "I know the facts, and I know Anita's heart," eventually I became welcome once again to sing, speak, or otherwise assist at various churches throughout the United States. From the beginning Vonette and Bill Bright of Campus Crusade for Christ had sent me loving and supportive messages through mutual friends.

I had always tithed my time, trying to answer church invitations if possible, glad to serve. My gratitude to James

Robison, who on his own initiative spoke in my behalf to other church leaders, cannot be properly expressed. Following my divorce, quite frankly, I felt like an outcast, no longer welcome to serve in church settings, an embarrassment to other Christians. I was cancelled by many churches when the news was splattered across the country. In time and through the grace of God, I have been restored to my natural sphere of activities in churches and other Christian groups. I praise God for Brother Robison and those men of God who followed him in serving as God's agent for healing me.

These are intimate subjects I'm discussing here. Humanly, I sometimes thought that well-known leading churchmen were all too willing to use me and even exploit me when I could *enhance* their services, but after the divorce, unwilling to touch me with a ten-foot pole.

More fairly, I always knew that America's finest church leaders, pastors, lay Christians and all who follow God's will, grapple every day with the effects of sin on human lives—divorce, addiction, child abuse, abandonment, wife battering, thefts, greed, corruption. . . .

I thought of Uncle Luther Berry, Mama's brother, who throughout his long ministry upheld God's principles so faithfully that, for scriptural reasons, he declined to preside at marriages of persons who had been divorced. I respected that, knowing my wonderful, loving uncle is not judgmental, but ever careful to carry out God's expectations as he understands them. Could I hate this Baptist pastor for his views on divorce? Never.

What, then, is the answer for those of us who sin and fall short? Are we to feel as hopeless, spiritually, as I did at first? That is where the grace of God begins to operate. Humbly, at the foot of the cross, with nothing whatever to recommend us, we begin to receive. We can do nothing at all for ourselves. We cannot explain or justify our circumstances. Often we feel wretched and worthless, and believe our restoration to be an impossibility. Thus, we limit God's power toward us.

Like Uncle Luther, his son, Rennie Berry, also grew up to serve God as an ordained Baptist minister. Imagine my surprise when my pastor cousin telephoned one day to request that I travel to his church in Kansas to help conduct a singles seminar.

"Me?" I stammered. "Are you sure?"

"Who better than you, Anita?" Rennie responded. "You've experienced the pain of divorce. Thousands and thousands of Christian people suffer that particular pain, and the church is failing them. I hope you'll come."

"Most churches treat divorce as the unforgivable sin," I told Rennie somewhat bitterly. "People like me feel there's no way back, certainly no way that the church stands ready to offer."

"You know God better than that," my cousin reproved me. "It might help you to come help us with this ministry."

Not only is Rennie Berry the sort of strong Christian pastor that I love and respect, but he is like a brother to me. We are family. We think a lot alike. There is mutual respect. More importantly, this is one person I have known all my life, and from whom I keep few secrets. He's a little crazy like me, too. I can get angry, not think before I speak, argue, tell Rennie off if I feel like it, yet nothing changes. He accepts me as I am. "You get on that plane and come," Rennie ordered. I went.

Scared as I was, wondering what I might say, fearing what others might think about me, wanting only to hide myself from other people's curiosity, despite all my fears, I accepted Rennie's invitation to come to his church's singles seminar and partake of the grace of God.

There are no words to describe the sweetness of that weekend as other Christian "becomers" like me shared, questioned, testified, worshiped, prayed, and loved God and one another. Every hour of the first singles seminar I ever had attended seemed to produce fresh revelations to me. I did more weeping than talking that weekend for every time I started to share, I began to cry—the words would not come—but everyone wept with me, understood my pain, and we all experienced from the Lord some healing in our fractured emotions.

By their actions toward me, I realized, Uncle Luther and Cousin Rennie had encouraged me to take my eyes off my own feelings of despair and unworthiness, and place them on our God of unfailing mercy. That seminar probably produced more healing in me than anyone else.

If my cousin Rennie Berry seems like my brother, and his wife, Janet, my sister, that's a lifelong blessing we enjoy whenever we have a chance to reunite with one another. Busy pastors can't always break away and travel, and my schedule has always restricted me. Sometimes you ache to be with your family. From whatever distance, you always remember how special each family member seems to you, and you miss them dreadfully.

What I did not realize at first, however, was that God has placed us in a limitless family, with brothers and sisters everywhere. Early on, for example, I "happened" to meet Russell McCraw, the Christian minister who helped me produce my first budget. From the instant that we met, I somehow was aware I would love Russell like a brother forever.

I do not love lightly. The Bible describes *agapé* love, a selfless kind of friendship that has eternal values, and Russell and I understood it immediately. A few years younger then me, slender and dignified, Russell McCraw seemed truly interested in me and my life. He involves himself with others. He cares about you, and you feel it. Beyond those qualities, Russell has the confidence, peace and excitement that seem to radiate from practicing Christians. From the first, Russell and I felt totally at home and comfortable together—brother and sister.

"Don't you think God loves a good joke?" Russell asked, as we toiled over my financial projections.

"What kind of joke?"

"That I, an ex-homosexual, would be the one you allow to help you, Anita Bryant, with your finances?"

"I don't see you as a former homosexual."

"That's because when you are in Christ Jesus, you become a new creation," Russell answered, seriously. "I know you can't imagine that I ever participated in that life-style. Frankly, I can't either. When God comes into your life, you change. It has been only a few years, and I still feel the same awe I felt when I turned myself and my life over to God."

"You couldn't have done it yourself, Russell," I reminded him, "but neither could any of the rest of us. I agree your life is a miracle, but so is mine. God's salvation represents a miracle in each life that receives it!"

God had removed Russell from a flamboyant Hollywood life-style, filled with glitzy parties, big-name friends, and expensive material possessions, via a perfectly natural means. He brought Russell face to face with a movie star at one of those parties, and that individual took occasion to witness to Russell about Jesus Christ.

"The following days were torment," Russell told me. "I had heard the truth, and I recognized it as the truth. The words from that celebrity's mouth followed me wherever I went. At last I fell to my knees in my apartment and gave my life to Jesus Christ."

Russell recognized that action required him to turn his back on everything and everyone associated with that old life-style. He had to remove himself from all of it, to follow Jesus Christ. "I felt desperate to know more about God," he told me. "There is a large group of film stars who actively witness for the Lord, who attend church, prayer meetings, and Bible-study groups. They helped me become fully involved and nurtured my spiritual growth.

Debby Boone and her husband Gabriel Ferrer, in particular, befriended and helped me."

Russell's search for God's will in his life led him to Tulsa, where we met again, and where he entered into Bible study and full-time preparation for Christian ministry.

Despite the many people who surrounded Russell—he has an attractive, interesting personality and is a lot of fun—I sensed that his life had reached as dramatic a crossroads as that of my own, and that he felt equally lonely at times.

Our paths crossed many times in Alabama and later in Atlanta, and we share a network of Christian friends. Russell McCraw and I have spent countless hours in prayer together, discussed things of the Spirit, and searched the Scriptures, but we also shared some lighter experiences—movies, dinner, shopping. Sometimes he stayed with my kids so I could run errands or meet an appointment. As our friendship deepened, Russell helped me understand why individuals can be seduced into a homosexual lifestyle, and how we can minister to them.

As Russell and I agreed many times, God's grace brought us together for a mutually beneficial brother-sister relationship. Russell helped me grow and encouraged me to minister to others; he led me to Ken Simmons, as he lay dying of AIDS. As for me, I supported Russell's Be Whole Ministries with my prayers and humble offerings, and have seen God use this man mightily.

How often I realize, *it is God who gives us grace to persevere*. During our stay in Selma, those years when I tried to hide, God had placed me in His crucible. Sometimes the loneliness and inner struggles seemed endless. Why? *Why?* Would life seem this pointless forever? Job's friend Elihu said that God "giveth songs in the night" (Job 35:10). Some nights, afflicted by insomnia, I would climb out of bed and grab a pen and paper. Without trying to think, I would begin to write a few words, a thought, a line of melody.

I didn't know I could write such songs. Never before had my life offered such spaces of time, nights when sleep would not come, days when the phone did not ring, evenings when nothing was planned.

Creativity requires solitude. Those apparently empty days and long nights actually provided a seedbed for fertile thoughts and dreams, as well as questions. The songs began to come more frequently. Sometimes I had to work for days before a verse or melody suited me. Other times they tumbled out of my mind like a perfect, just-born baby.

One summer day in Selma I sat in my backyard, alone except for the bees that buzzed from petunia to petunia, with a chorus of birds for backup. Somewhere a wind chime tinkled. I tilted my lawn chair so I could lean back and study the dazzlingly green pine trees, their needles sparkling in the sun like thousands of emeralds. I fixed my eyes and my mind on this beauty and thought about absolutely nothing else. Just that simply, a new song formed within me. I had to hurry into the house and grab some writing materials before it all vanished.

That's how God gave me the song I called "The Pines of Alabama." That scene stands out in my memory as a little piece of near perfection, an experience to treasure, but no other song arose from such peace.

Indeed my next song, which arrived some weeks later, sprang from a seedbed of anguish. I had once loved a man whose critical spirit often ate into me like acid. He was in town, and we had quarreled badly, with a fallout of emotional acid rain which filled me with self-hatred. That morning, alone at home and hurting, I turned to God. I cried out. "Jesus, how long do I continually have to receive this condemnation?" A quiet voice seemed to whisper in my thought patterns, "When you're ready to give it up." Shocked at the thought, I spoke out loud, "Satan must be involved in this self-hatred."

So I prayed for the Lord to bind the enemy and prayed once more the same prayer, and much to my surprise the same gentle words crossed my mind, "When you're ready to give up receiving the condemnation!" With no hesitation, I said, "I'm ready now!" The verse, Romans 8:1, came to mind: "There is therefore now _no condemnation_ to them which are in Christ Jesus, who walk not after the flesh, but after the Spirit" (author's italics). From that day forward I no longer _received_ condemnation. It didn't keep other individuals from _giving_ condemnation, but God had settled it in _my_ heart and mind.

I had been in a tape study by Kay Arthur, who has a ministry in Chattanooga, Tennessee, on the apostle Paul (1 Cor. 15:10), and out of it came a song of accepting myself. Deep within my soul, words began to form themselves into sequence, and a melody fitted itself to the words.

God gave a song to His daughter who felt so mute, so unable to sing. I prayed. I wrote. Some time later, I telephoned a friend because I had to tell someone what had just happened.

My friend was in a hurry. I felt embarrassed, but asked, awkwardly, "Would you indulge me? Could I sing this song that God just gave me?"

"Sure," she answered, somewhat indifferently. She had her own problems; her husband had asked her for a divorce. I probably should have called someone else.

She let me sing the song—the first verse, at least, which was all I had at the time. We both sensed that more would come. There was a long, long silence. "Are you there?" I asked. Then I heard the quiet weeping, and her broken voice saying, "Anita, God sent that song to me. I just told Him I couldn't stand one more thing, and He _had_ to speak to me or I would simply crack up!"

That song brings tears whenever I sing it, for every audience understands its message—"I Am What I Am by the Grace of My God." These words are straight out of Scripture. By now I understood full well that God's grace often manifested itself to me in song. Some, like that one, sprang from the Scriptures, or from praise. Others were less serious, romantic, or even funny.

I could not seem to "make" a song, but merely waited for each to appear. I somehow felt that God deliberately caused each one to happen at precisely the right time. I wrote them down, sang them to myself occasionally, and stored them in a drawer to wait, for what?

Much later, I was to learn how the songs I wrote, those He gave me, could be used. Meanwhile, each one, like the precious and significant gift it was, gave me grace to persevere and strength to go forward with Him.

Some people protested my working to raise funds for the Statue of Liberty/Ellis Island Foundation. "She is bigoted and un-American," my critics hollered. Chairman Lee Iacocca paid little attention to the dissenters, and I was allowed to continue my efforts. I needed to participate in that national effort, whatever the criticism. I determined not to allow my detractors to sidetrack me.

Imagine my amazement, then, the day I received the New York Statue of Liberty telegram. Elaborate dedication ceremonies honoring the restored Lady Liberty were in the works. How I wished I could afford to attend!

"Congratulations!" I read aloud to myself. "The people of America have chosen you as a recipient of the congressionally sponsored Ellis Island Medal of Honor. This award honors the contributions of individuals from each of the major heritage groups that comprise the nation's population.

"Nominations were made by the public through a series of newspaper, television, and radio announcements. Winners were selected by the National Ethnic Coalition of Organizations (NECO). (I learned later that my friend Bob Hope had also nominated me.)

"Your Medal of Honor will be awarded at a presentation on Ellis Island at noon, Monday, October 27, 1986. . . ."

I read and reread the telegram, stunned by the facts that had begun to sink in: I *would* attend the ceremonies, would have a ringside seat, in fact, for the prayers, the bands, the speeches, participating with many of America's most famous people. I also was invited to attend the July Fourth celebration and experience firsthand the tall ships, the fireworks, all the essence of our nation's partiotic fervor.

Tears filled my eyes as I thought about the Medal of Honor, to be presented to "outstanding American citizens who have distinguished themselves in their respective fields of endeavor, while preserving the values of their particular heritage groups." Jacqueline Kennedy Onassis, Gregory Peck, Cardinal Spellman, Barbara Walters, Bob Hope, Victor Borge, Walter Cronkite, Joe DiMaggio, Claudette Colbert, Coretta Scott King, altogether some eighty Americans representing various nations, including "Anita Bryant, singer, Native American." While there I had the joy of being with Kathie Lee Gifford, one of my best encouragers. She is co-host with Regis Philbin of "Live with Regis and Kathie Lee." I immediately called Dad to thank him for his Indian heritage to me. I often jokingly complained of inheriting his big hands and feet, so it delighted him to hear some positive comments on the Bryant bloodline. Unquestionably, God had done this thing which held such great meaning to me. Once again, I recognized His grace and power to restore. There *is* room in America for an Anita Bryant.

One reporter later wrote: "Anita Bryant sported a yellow corsage, a pink hat, and a colorful spring dress Friday. The attire was Easter-like, and for her the event certainly was a resurrection of sorts.

"After eight years of relative obscurity the former Florida citrus sweetheart emerged Friday as the very first woman, and youngest, to be inducted into the Florida Citrus Hall of Fame."

Though the reporter may have considered it just another industry story, those words depicted God's awesome favor to me. Eight years earlier much of the American public identified me with my role as a spokesperson for the Florida Citrus Commission. Advertising experts credited the liaison with putting the Florida citrus industry on the map, setting advertising records, and sending sales zooming. With my husband and children, I had been featured in their advertising. Anita Bryant became synonymous with orange juice.

For me, the best part of that work was being friends with the citrus growers. Most were Christians, active in church and community. I loved them and their families, and they loved us. We shared common values.

When the controversy about Anita Bryant peaked, one sponsor after another canceled my bookings, but the Florida Citrus Commission stood behind me. Many of the individual growers offered strong support. At last, however, their advertising agency prevailed upon the Commission not to renew my contract. I had become "too controversial." That decision caved me in, not only financially, but personally.

Suddenly, after eleven years with little contact with the growers and none with the Commission, the telephone call came from John Baldwin, a longtime friend and Citrus Ad Agency associate. "Anita, they would like to induct you into the Florida Citrus Hall of Fame. You will become the first woman and the youngest person ever to receive this honor."

That moment absolutely flabbergasted me. I accepted eagerly, and invited my younger daughter, Barbara, to accompany me to the ceremonies. Barbara had been a dimpled preteen when the growers last had seen her, and I thought it would be fun to introduce at least one of my young grownups who once were featured in their ads.

The entire occasion represented nothing but fun and healing, a wonderful reunion with the men and women who conduct one of Florida's most important industries. Old friends like William Strickland, who founded the Florida Citrus Packers, and J. J. Parrish, Jr., a former citrus commissioner, greeted, escorted, and made over us. Jerry Chicone, head of the Florida Citrus Showcase, and dear friends, Bill and Thelma Raley, hosted us in their home and gave us an elegant private dinner with a few citrus-industry friends. Also present were faithful friends Dolly and George King and the Bazemores. We had a joyous party throughout the Hall of Fame induction luncheon. It was filled with laughing, hugging, and catching up. And of course I sang, "Come to the Florida Sunshine Tree!"—receiving a standing ovation.

Even Barbara understood what God had done. Her blonde hair and green eyes seemed to shine even more than usual as old friends exclaimed about my little girl grown up, and I beamed with pleasure. "Thank You, Lord," my heart continued to sing. As I write about this, I marvel again at the faithfulness of God. By His love and grace, we become restored. The broken places in our lives become not merely mended, but brand-new.

"Thank You, Father, that you let my sensitive little Barbara see this, too," I told Him. "In the fullness of time, You make everything come full circle."

Like David, I can tell you with confidence, "He hath put a new song in my mouth, even praise unto our God: many shall see it, and fear, and shall trust in the Lord" (Ps. 40:3).

11
Because I Really Need You

*A*gain my mind returned to our bittersweet days in Selma. Women, chattering and hugging, poured into the meeting room in Birmingham, Alabama, where Christian fellowship was about to begin. I sat on the front row, dressed in dark clothes and sunglasses, hoping no one would approach me. I had not met those women, but drove over from Selma that morning with one of my girl friends, Carolyn Dobbs, to hear the speaker, who is another longtime friend. I forced myself to make this effort to support her.

However, I soon wished I had stayed at home. The meeting began with praise and worship, and to my shock, I did not know one single song! The enthusiastic singing swirled around me as I stood mute, trying to look as though I were singing, too. Apparently someone had set Scripture verses to music; also, there were some beautiful choruses of adoration to Jesus. The girl who led the singing attracted me. *Obviously she had not been musically trained,* I thought critically, yet she sang with such joy and spontaneity that she could have led a stone to worship. *Who was she,* I wondered, *and where did she get those songs?*

It wasn't that I decided to reach out to others. It was more like willing to be willing to enter some unknown situations, and that does not necessarily mean you will feel comfortable when you do. Nothing about that service felt comfortable until my friend began to speak, and until we sang "Amazing Grace." Yes, I was familiar with that favorite old hymn of the church!

When the speaker concluded the group began to pray. *Good,* I thought. *In a few minutes we can get away to lunch. It's almost over.*

Wrong! Almost immediately one of the girls approached me. "You're Anita Bryant," she said in a shy voice, "and I want to tell you I love you. Please don't let me intrude, but I want you to know how much you have been in my prayers these past months."

Quietly, still in a prayer mode, some of the other women encircled me. "May we pray for you?" one asked.

To my horror, I burst into tears. One set of arms after another offered gentle hugs as the group quietly prayed, and my sobs grew noisier and noisier. I could not stop crying, yet it did not seem to matter. Some of the other women, older ones as well as younger, also quietly cried. Dismayed as I felt about all this and as much as I hated it, the strong feeling of God's powerful presence in that room swept over each of us. It felt OK to let go and honestly express my pain.

Soon we began sharing with one another. Someone mentioned the praise leader and called her over for prayer. Then I learned that this beautiful young woman had been widowed just two months earlier. "How can you sing?" I asked her. I shall never forget her answer. "Whenever I try to serve Him, He strengthens me," she replied simply. Then she said, "Anita, I've been praying for you ever since your divorce, and felt much of your pain, and I've come to the conclusion that death of a loved one is far easier than divorce. Death is final, but divorce has to be dealt with continually, especially if there are children involved.

"I will be faithful to pray for you and your family in the days ahead." Her wisdom and faith amazed and humbled me also, as I thought of her loss only two months before.

The fellowship that morning felt so sweet, and I had

been starved for it. My sunglasses came off, my makeup was a mess, and tears continually flooded my eyes, but I just didn't care. How many long months had it been since I felt such release? How much I needed these women!

Later several of us lunched together, bubbling over with conversation and laughter. I felt as though I had known them all my life. Nevertheless, a bit of nervousness was rising within me because I was about to do something I never had done before. I had promised a friend in Selma that I would visit a Birmingham woman, his former secretary, to pray for her. LaVere, whom I had not met, suffered a terminal illness. Her doctors had exhausted all possible medical approaches to her problem. Throughout lunch I silently prayed for LaVere, and asked Jesus, the Divine Physician, to touch her.

Though praying for the sick was not new to me, this time I believed God was asking me to anoint her with oil as we are instructed to do in the final verses of the Book of James. Certainly there was no magic in the oil, but it symbolizes the healing love and power of God's Holy Spirit. As an act of obedience, I intended to do everything the Scripture described.

Sometime during the lunch I asked the other women if they had ever anointed and prayed for a sick person. To my surprise, each one there was experienced in such one-on-one ministry and even offered to go with me, if I wished.

LaVere did not seem to mind at all that five gals instead of one trooped into her pretty bedroom. We read James's words about healing, chatted with her for a few moments, then anointed LaVere, and prayed the prayer of faith. All my nervousness vanished, of course, as God's sweetness flowed through our little group and helped us pray as one person.

We did not stay long. I remember LaVere's pale face, radiant and smiling as she told us, "The pain is gone!" Propped up on lacy pillows and dressed in a dainty bed jacket, LaVere did not look sick, only peaceful and happy.

That day represented a major milestone in my determination to allow God to use me however and wherever He would. *I had so little to give,* I thought. In fact, I could hardly remember when I felt truly capable and at my best—vigorous and "up" and filled with enthusiasm. Maybe I never would feel that way again. Whatever my feelings, however, I recognized God's gentle nudgings whenever opportunities arose for me to serve.

You can't merely wait until you *feel* like serving God. Attending that meeting, quite honestly, was much more of an effort than I really cared to make. Still, I am loyal to my friends; sometimes I will do things for them I would not do for myself.

That day I learned that when we put forth our puny little effort, God responds in unforgettable ways. I intended to support my girl friend and LaVere, but ended up receiving major ministry for myself. As our songleader told me, the tiniest act of giving somehow strengthens us, and that happens every time. We cannot wait for some far-off day when we truly feel ready to love and serve; that day may never come, for all we know. When we decide, despite our pain, to give our emotional and physical widow's mite, God begins to work mighty miracles in our lives.

Giving from our weakness builds our strength. Giving from our financial need creates wealth. Giving from our heart and from our obedience engenders joy. I certainly would not imply that we should give in order to get, but there is a principle here. We cannot outgive God.

As my dear friend Jean Norment once explained to me, whenever we love, give, or serve, we act as Jesus acts, and thus we take on His love, peace, and joy. We become His earthly agents. As Jean said, "When Jesus wants to give somebody a hug, He has to use your arms."

When we look to God to lead us in our daily lives, He guides us at times with almost imperceptible inner nudges which often lead us to certain people. When we genuinely interact with others, especially those we may not know at all, we can experience some exciting encounters.

Knowing LaVere and watching her Christian courage taught me so much about how to live this life while we prepare to enter the next. LaVere saw it as *graduation,* and approached it with strength and zest. She ministered to me far more than I did to her.

Those were the days when few familiar faces surrounded me. I could either find new friends, God clearly showed me, or stay out of step. I often seesawed between wanting to obey God and feeling too emotionally drained to make the effort. But even when we hate to make any effort, we never regret shaking off our lethargy to follow the Lord's leading!

I smile to think about the assorted group of straggling strugglers who assembled at my house in Selma when the Lord first led me to form a singles one-on-one ministry. Spiritually, we seemed all "arms and legs." We came from several different denominations. Some felt ill at ease. Many never had prayed aloud or shared their thoughts in a group. At first it seemed it would not work. I felt almost embarrassed at our efforts.

"Have I stepped out ahead of you again, Jesus?" I asked. "It sure wouldn't be the first time! Can a divorced woman like me have anything at all to offer other divorced or hurting people?"

We kept trying. When the group grew larger we met on Sunday mornings at a motel coffee shop before attending our respective churches. The tone changed. Friendships were forged, prayer partners began to pray for specific needs in one another's lives during the coming week, and we saw several powerful answers to prayer. None of us can grasp the eternal significance of our banding together.

One day one of our partners—I'll call her Wanda—happened to ride with me to do some errands in Birmingham. On our way in the van, at a certain stretch of the road, this dear woman's body tensed, and her face looked stricken as she stared ahead through the windshield. I thought she might be about to suffer some kind of seizure.

"What's wrong?" I asked.

"Nothing," she replied in a strangely agitated voice.

"Should I pull over and stop?" I urged, wondering if I remembered my first-aid training. I felt terribly scared.

"No! Keep going, please don't stop. I'm all right," she answered, though obviously that was not so. I prayed hard, and God seemed to tell me to keep driving. Wanda slowly relaxed. Only over lunch did she tell me what happened. "My husband killed himself, leaving me and our three sons," she told me. "He pulled over to the side of the road and walked into the woods and shot himself. It has been two years, but every time I pass that spot I experience a panic attack. I can't help it," she said, as tears spilled from her eyes. "Will I ever get over that?"

"Let's pray right now," I suggested. Taking Wanda's hands in mine I prayed quietly, there in our restaurant booth. To my relief, she seemed much better.

I may have dreaded our return trip even more than Wanda did. As we headed toward Selma, I began to pray silently. Wanda sat quiet and still, huddled close to the window. "Relax her, Lord," I prayed. "Please heal her memories. Take away the horror."

Soon my van almost seemed to steer itself to the side of the road. "Where are we going?" Wanda asked in a faint voice. "Across the road," I told her.

"Please! No!" Her voice sounded pitiful, pleading.

"Wanda, we must. God does not want you to live with that fear and torment, and you don't have to," I heard myself saying. "We are going to stand on that spot and pray for God to deliver you from that curse."

Wanda's white face and wide eyes almost swayed me, but this was God's idea, not mine. I was assured there was no turning back, but I did wonder what to do once we arrived at the place that saddened Wanda so.

I should not have doubted God. A subdued Wanda mutely pointed to the spot "where it happened," and we stood there. I took her hands in mine and prayed, silently praying also that nobody would stop and ask what we were doing. Nobody stopped. Firmly and thoroughly, I rebuked Satan, that thief who comes to steal, kill, and destroy, and asked our loving Heavenly Father to heal Wanda's emotions and give her the peace that passes all understanding. Within moments we were able to cross the road and head toward home, literally and figuratively.

One rich legacy Teddy Heard left me and countless others was her knowledge of group synergy—the fact that the whole group can become far greater than the sum of its imperfect parts. Teddy possessed a genius for interacting with other people with such superb interest and love that each went away feeling somehow better than before. One reason is, Teddy continually studied human relations, considering all her friendships and other encounters as divine opportunities.

At night, Teddy often crawled out of bed and wrote pages of notes about problems, people, and answers and insights she gleaned when she prayed and thought. Those writings excited her. Sometimes she'd phone and read last night's ideas in her inimitable Texas drawl until I burst out laughing, and she began to laugh at my laughter. Teddy, you did talk funny!

She sent me a number of those pages, and I reread them from time to time, always marveling at the wisdom God gave such a young woman. (Teddy was less than forty when she went to be with our Lord.) Here is one of the "jewels" Teddy wrote and gave me: now I pass it along to you.

"I used to think of 'Christ in you' as somehow _separate_ from you, living Himself somewhere 'in' you. But in relationships I am discovering that I experience 'Christ in you' as *the Source* of your personality's vitality, *the Essence* of your intellect's constant probing, *the Dynamics* of your being's impact on me. 'Christ in you' is the beautiful infusing process of His life and strength through your being, in such a way that you actually experience and recognize His life as the *wellspring* of your being and yearn for a deeper dimension of His glory yourself. This yearning urges me to be for someone else what you are to me."

I believe those words were written in the early 1970s as Teddy thought of her husband, Houston Judge Wyatt Heard, but they can instruct each of us. What better friend can you have than someone who teaches you so much about friendship?

While living in Atlanta I became friends with Max Cleland, presently secretary of state for the state of Georgia and former director of the Veterans Administration during President Carter's term, has taught all those who come in contact with him about triumph over terrible personal tragedy.

Max is a consummate "people person." As a young Army captain in Vietnam, he saw a grenade lying on the ground, and without thinking, picked it up so none of his men would be harmed. That action cost Max both legs and his right arm. For most people, it might also have cost the government career he had trained himself to achieve.

Friends say Max Cleland not only refused to die, but during even his first agonizing days at Walter Reed Hospital in Washington, D.C., wheeled his chair from room to room to help build other patients' morale. It worked. That decision helped other patients, and it also helped Max. The Army officer's instincts—to disregard oneself and look out for others—served to keep Max Cleland from quitting the battle. He healed. He helped others around him. He enjoys life to the fullest and has built a career of distinguished public service.

If Max in serving our nation's Army built such concern and responsibility for others into his character that those habits prevailed, even when it seemed he had lost nearly everything, what does that show those of us who have both legs and serve as foot soldiers in the Army of God? How much more should we be willing to step forward and serve others for our Lord's sake? Therein we lose ourselves in order to find it all.

Reaching out . . .

In my life, that had often meant entertaining. To offer one's words or songs is to give as much of oneself as possible to the hearer, always hoping that what you offer is worthy to be received. I did not miss my career or even my singing, but I did miss the communication they afforded.

Then came the terrifying decision that I would cut some new recordings. Since recording campanies no longer cared to promote Anita Bryant records, my advisers had worked out a direct-mail program which would bypass those obstructions.

Imagine the nervousness with which I prepared myself to cut the first two albums in ten years. I felt all my friends were praying for me. Could I still sing? Could I stand the pressure? Would the albums sell?

Seth Marshall stayed cool. My secretary Julia and he made all the business arrangements, engaged top backup artists, and found a fine Hollywood recording studio. We flew out early for some voice coaching, rehearsals, and photo sessions. I also made a couple of television appearances that week, just to be sure I wasn't completely idle!

Truthfully, I looked forward to the recording sessions with some reluctance. More than those, however, I shrank from my sessions with the vocal coach. I had not had formal training or much coaching since childhood, and the more I thought about it, the more I became convinced that this professional coach probably would find so much wrong with my singing methods that I would end up not recording at all.

That wasn't the real reason, though. Many years earlier one of the many professionals who worked with me had subjected me to what I now recognize was sexual harassment. I dreaded those "opportunities" to be around him, and those ancient, buried fears had begun to surface. As my first vocal appointment approached I actually felt panic.

I prayed. I found another Christian, spilled the story, and we prayed together. She and Seth sat in the car while I went in to vocalize. As I sang, they prayed, and the most astonishing thing happened. "You really don't need any coaching at all, Anita," my instructor said. "Except for one or two little suggestions, I really don't think you need me."

I ran out of that studio praising God. The ensuing recording sessions turned out to be fun. The musicians were so fine, their music so wonderful, and I loved the songs I was recording. (I even loved the songs I wrote, several of which appear on the Christian album, in particular.) At last God had led me to what I considered the outer limits of my personal "reaching out." Those songs were recorded for you, and the album title says it all: "Anita, With Love."

P. S. I had no idea how those new albums would be received, but again God humbled and amazed me. "Her voice has matured into an even greater instrument than that of her younger days," one critic wrote. Gradually it began to dawn on me that singing is not simply a job, but I really need to sing. I have something to give, but I must be willing to reach towards you, first.

As Teddy wrote to one of her many friends, "You have

struck me at a deep, deep level and have challenged me to be myself in a way I never dared. This in turn is giving me more courage to allow others the freedom to respond to me more authentically."

This can happen when we find the courage to reach out to others, being conscious that we need one another.

12
To Love Again

"I guess it's not in God's plan for me ever to be happily married," I commented to a friend. "That's not scriptural," she disagreed. "God says it's not good for mankind to live alone. He sets the solitary in families. How could you believe what you just said?"

I shook my head. "I've read those Scriptures, but I'm convinced," I replied. At that time I was very much in love with a man who did not want to marry me or anyone else. Tremendously negative feelings arose in me whenever I thought about the possibility of ever experiencing deep love and marital fulfillment. "Why should God bless me with a husband?" I asked. "What have I done to deserve real happiness? Nothing."

Such arguments did not impress my Christian friends. "God wants the very best for you," one gal after another reminded me. "None of us *deserve* His blessings, after all. Do you really believe that God loves you?"

Neither Scripture nor prayer budged those negative feelings, nor could anyone argue them away. Often alone (the man I cared for lived in another state, so our courtship consisted of daily telephone contacts and infrequent visits) I began to feel burdened by the lack of momentum in my personal life. As I struggled to rebuild my career, I could not deny that the deeply personal and feminine side of myself seemed always to tread water. I told myself that he was worth waiting for, and whenever our love drew us marvelously close I *knew* God eventually would give me the desire of my heart. It just required patience on my part, I reasoned, and faith. How I prayed for more faith!

Other days, after a spat or a disappointment, a bleak negativism settled over me. *Marriage is not in my future,* I thought. *There is no husband for me.* Then I would address myself to the tasks required to push my career forward, thinking with a hint of bitterness that some people applauded the public side of me, but rejected the real person. No wonder I could not whip up a lot of enthusiasm about returning to show business!

For months, two sides of myself, career woman versus private person, battled each other. "The woman, wife, and mother in me always have to take a backseat," I told God. "Aren't those aspects of me important to You at all? Lord, Anita Jane the woman keeps making stronger and stronger efforts to emerge . . . and meanwhile, God, even Your Christian servants sometimes use and abuse the public side of me. It's as though the singer is all some people ever accept. When I risk pushing my womanly self forward it's like casting pearls before swine. The real me keeps getting trampled."

I could hardly express these strong emotions, yet I also found it impossible to stuff them down. My private battles became even more frustrating as I faced the complex stresses produced by all my attempts to make a living. "God has not equipped women to handle the pressures of being the main breadwinner," I exclaimed in total exasperation. "I want to be married and need to be married, but I'm in love with a man who refuses to commit to marriage."

How can anyone become so emotionally entangled with someone who sincerely does not feel equipped for matrimony? Obviously, the man I cared for was a fine person, or I would not have loved him. Clearly he loved and respected me, yet would not consider marriage to me.

Actually, there was little mystery to my quandary;

many another divorced man or woman finds himself or herself on one side or the other of that same hurtful puzzle. It may be because we still feel too hurt to trust someone new. Or subconsciously we may choose to love someone who can't commit to us because, despite the pain, it makes us feel safe. We become emotionally deadlocked. The relationship remains exactly as it is, one that probably must die of attrition since it cannot grow into marriage.

I experienced two such relationships following my divorce. Each man was someone I respected as well as loved. Both were high-profile achievers, sophisticated, and attractive, but more importantly, both were Christians who respected my faith. There were other nice men in my life as well, but those two relationships involved years of my life and shut out any possibility of other friendships developing beyond stage one.

My first love relationship came too soon following my divorce. It moved thrillingly quick; soon we were making marriage plans and had entered into premarital counseling. It felt glorious to experience love again with a mature and exciting man who obviously admired and enjoyed me. So we moved steadily closer to marriage, or so I believed, until one day I was jolted into reality. I should have seen it coming, when at the last minute he backed out of marriage three different times, but love is so blind. I had been living in a fool's paradise.

That day my beloved telephoned me from another city to tell me, with tears, that he had just married another woman. I had been told several days prior, but didn't believe he would go through with it. He offered no real explanation, and the sweet dreams he led me to believe we had, vanished and turned into the horrible end of a nightmare. The tabloids splashed it all over: "Anita Bryant Dumped by Fiancée for a Younger Woman." To put it mildly, it devastated me. My entire family was hurt, and I went into shock. It took months of excruciating anguish before I could recover from my deep depression and suicidal thoughts. Sometimes when we're desperate for love and marriage (the old curse again), our own desires can rationalize all kinds of situations, claiming it's God's plan for us when all the while we have been deceived into carrying out our willful ways, which in the end can only bring death in a relationship, not new life.

Why should I reveal such things? I do not enjoy sharing them, but must spell out the facts truthfully in order to reveal the faithfulness of God. It required time for me to acknowledge that God had allowed the tragic breakup I have just described to deliver me from a potentially disastrous premature marriage. At the time, I felt certain that my heart had been irreparably broken. I could not admit even to myself that someone capable of such irresponsibility could ever build a strong marriage with me or anyone else. I loved him and made excuses for his behavior.

It is not at all unusual for men and women who have suffered divorce to leave themselves open to the sort of experience I went through. Perhaps, like me, they married young and had little knowledge about the opposite sex. Perhaps we were naïve. Or likely, there is the possibility that our emotions became so unbalanced by years of unhappiness and the brutal ending divorce placed on our years of marital investment, that we can't think straight. We feel starved for love, approval, companionship, sex, security, emotional gratification, encouragement, status in society, help with rearing our children, respect from our peers, and everything else marriage is supposed to provide, but all too often doesn't. We just want a normal life! Sometimes we settle for a "good relationship" when God's perfect plan and God's perfect timing would provide us with "the *best* relationship."

I went from the emotional frying pan into the fire. My first dashed hopes were soon replaced by my affections for another man who despised the way my first love had treated me, and who offered, by contrast, every attention, respect, and courtesy. In my eyes he seemed nearly perfect. I devoted myself to his spiritual and emotional welfare and prayed earnestly that God would bring us together. Instead, the relationship ran its course as I tried desperately to keep it alive, to no avail.

"Why, God?" I wept. "Who could be more perfect for me? We're dear friends, and he would take care of me, I wouldn't have to work outside the home, and I'm good for him as well. Is it wrong for me to want to love and be loved?"

As that second relationship struggled to survive, I attended a meaningful Christian seminar directed by John and Paula Sandford, the noted Christian psychologists and prayer warriors. Coauthors of the best-selling book, _The Transformation of the Inner Man,_ the Sandfords also facilitate many powerful inner healings as God leads them in one-on-one ministry. These precious people and I intersected at a key moment in my life. I felt barren, desolate, and hopeless. Aside from more work, it often seemed that life had little else to offer. Nearly eight years had elapsed since my divorce, and though each day brought many reasons to praise God and count His many blessings to me, I confess that bitterness began to creep into my heart whenever I considered the idea that somehow I had forfeited all hope of marriage.

At the end of their seminar, I introduced myself to the Sandfords and arranged to meet them for private consultation. I desperately hoped they could help me break up my emotional logjam. I needed healing and hope and answers for my life.

Almost immediately, Agnes Sandford discerned a major part of my fractured feelings. "You must accept yourself as a performer," she told me. "It's as though the singer Anita Bryant and the woman Anita Jane have become enemies, but the performer is just as valid as any other part of the person you are.

"Accept yourself as a performer," she said. "Love that part of yourself, too!"

Then began a period in which Agnes Sandford skillfully and prayerfully guided me into understanding much about the maze my inner life had become. During our sessions we asked God to help me work through some painfully dark areas of my emotions—my parents' divorce when I was very young, which resulted in my separation from my father; and later, as a budding starlet, the sexual harassment I was too inexperienced to fend off, which left me feeling dirty and ashamed as though it were my fault.

Satan has robbed so many of us of those parts of our lives so fundamental to self-love and self-respect. Jesus said, "The thief cometh not, but for to steal, and to kill, and to destroy: I am come that they might have life, and that they might have it more abundantly" (John 10:10). I began to realize that Satan would like to rob me of the joy of singing, in addition to all else.

But if the thief comes to steal and destroy, how much more does our Heavenly Father heal the broken places in our lives? Neither my own sins, the sins of my parents or other authority figures, nor any other creature, can separate me from the love of Christ!

John and Agnes helped me see that we indeed are "fearfully and wonderfully made," but that God could heal my life and yours and make us every whit whole in mind, body, and spirit. Inner healing may occur quickly, but often is a long process. Hurts which transpire over a period of time are healed over time, as we allow the Holy Spirit to work.

Though such dynamic Christian counseling did much to help me understand more about the personality forces which shape our lives, one fact still did not change: I wanted the man I loved. I yearned for God to incline his heart toward marriage, so he would realize how perfect we could be as husband and wife.

A New Day

I agreed with the Sandfords that my primary goal
should be that of allowing God to help me mature into a
stronger Christian woman. But at the same time, couldn't
I pray a similar prayer for my counterpart? And perhaps,
wouldn't that mean we might even be married someday,
in God's time?

You know the rest of that story. That marriage was not
to be, but God replaced my hope with an amazing devel-
opment as He began to work out a thorough restoration
process within my inner life. I became able to relinquish
some of my chief desires, including my fixation on marriage and the longing I felt for that particular man. I became truly open to God's guidance as to career decisions,
and tried to follow His lead more closely. On one level it
appeared that my life was in a shambles; on another level,
I recognized it had started to fit together as never before.

The Book of Nehemiah describes the trials and tri-
umphs of those Israelites engaged in rebuilding their city
walls, which had been destroyed by their enemies, leaving them exposed to every kind of terror and danger. This
symbolizes the work of God's Holy Spirit as He rebuilds
the walls of our human spirits, no matter how extensive
the damage.

Stone by stone, our lives can be rebuilt to greater
strengths and taller heights than before. I could feel it
happening in my own life as I recognized new quickening
and empowerment from God. Sure I still struggled, but I
also had that perfect peace that comes when you place
your hope and confidence in Jesus Christ. Real proof of
what God had done was manifested when the man I so
wished to marry and I mutually agreed to step back from
our old relationship. The decision was very difficult and
scary, but it did not kill me after all. There was sadness,
but also peace and tranquillity. I had placed marriage and
all my desires on God's altar, and for the first time since
my divorce told the Lord I was really willing finally to go
on alone with Him.

I could not imagine what God might have in store for me during the coming years of my life, but I anticipated with brand-new certainty that it would be good.

"Life is Good," reads the following statement which someone placed in my hands. Perhaps it will say as much to you as it did to me.

"Everyone longs to give themselves completely to someone . . . to have a deep soul relationship with another . . . to be loved thoroughly and completely. But God to a Christian says, 'No, not until you are satisfied, fulfilled, and content with being loved by Me alone—with giving yourself totally and unreservedly to Me; to having an intensely personal and unique relationship with Me alone; discovering that only in Me is your satisfaction to be found—will you be capable of the perfect human relationship that I have planned for you.

" 'You will never be united with another until you are united with Me . . . exclusive of anyone or anything else, exclusive of any other desires or longings. I want you to stop planning, stop wishing, and allow Me to give you the most thrilling plan there is . . . one you cannot imagine.

" 'I want you to have the best. Please allow Me to bring it to you. You just keep watching Me, expecting the greatest things. Keep experiencing the satisfaction that I am. Keep listening and learning the things I tell you. Just wait, that's all. Don't be anxious. Do not worry. Do not look around at the things others have, or that I have given them. Do not look at things you think you want. Just keep looking to Me, or you will miss what I want to show you. Then, when you are ready, I will surprise you with a love far more wonderful than any you could dream of.

" 'You see, until you are ready, and until the one I have for you is ready (I am working even at this moment to have both of you ready at the same time), until you both are satisfied exclusively with Me and the life I have prepared for you, you won't be able to experience the love that exemplifies your relationship with Me, and thus is perfect love.

"'Dear one, I want you to have this most wonderful love. I want you to see in the flesh a picture of your relationship with each other, and to enjoy materially and concretely the everlasting union of beauty, perfection, and love that I offer you with Myself. Know that I love you utterly. Believe it and be satisfied.'"

—Author Unknown

"I will surprise you with a love. . . ." Those words must have been written to me. Far sooner than I dreamed, the man arrived, the man God planned for me to love forever. At first, of course, neither he nor I suspected, so quietly and smoothly did God's plan work. My mind by now was not directed to the possibility of marriage, but was focused on an upcoming move I believed God was leading me to make just for me and my career, since Bobby and Gloria were now married, and Billy and Barbara were in college. In the summer of 1989 I relocated to America's music capital, Nashville, Tennessee. With country and western music, gospel, television specials, recording studios galore, Nashville has become a legendary crossroads for every star-struck hopeful who has a song to sing.

By now I had *songs,* the many varied songs God had given me, almost enough for a gospel and a country love album. My heart told me the time had come to record those songs. Where better than Nashville? Obviously, it was time to move.

Not long before my projected moving date, an old friend phoned me. "Anita? This is Charlie. Charlie Dry. Remember that business plan I told you about more than a year ago . . . the one you said you'd take a look at? Well, it's ready now. I'm eager for you to look it over. Any possibility I could come in this weekend?"

We agreed to meet, and Charlie flew in from Oklahoma. I looked forward to seeing him, because Charlie and I, my sister Sandy, and others in our family go way back. In fact, Charlie had been one of my first sweethearts. Summers when Sandy and I visited Grandpa and Grandma Berry in Tishomingo, Oklahoma, Charlie Dry entered the picture early on. His dad owned Chuck's Grocery on Main Street, and Charlie delivered groceries to Grandpa and Grandma, balancing the bags carefully on the handlebars of his bicycle or later in a yellow Jeep. He was ten and I was nine the summer we decided we were "in love," and our parents and grandparents allowed us to play together as much as possible. My folks thought Charlie was a nice boy, and his parents liked me, too.

Over forty years beyond that first innocent summer romance, Charlie Dry and I sat in my Atlanta kitchen and talked about his business. That cute, shy grocery boy had grown up to become a nuclear physicist. For eighteen years he had served as an Aerospace Engineer and Astronaut Test Crewman for NASA. I glanced at the highly trained and disciplined man who sat opposite me, long legs stuck straight out before him as always, hands gesturing, his voice alive, and his eyes dancing as they used to when he became excited, and I wondered. . . .

"Charlie, remember that old yellow Jeep you used to drive?"

"Yep, Dad let me have it when I was twelve. Put blocks on the pedals so my legs would reach. I delivered groceries to your grandpa in that thing."

"I know you did. You used to take me on dates in it, remember?"

"Sure do. I'd drive you to the game preserve and we'd count geese. . . ." We laughed, but I thought about that brash young boy and wondered. Who could have imagined that someday he would help send men into space? Had there been any sign that Charlie Dry would grow up to become so daring, focused, creative, and gutsy?

"Say, what do you think of my business proposal?" he asked me.

"Charlie, it looks great, but you know I'll have to study it. This subject is totally foreign to me." The truth was, Charlie's projected business plan had hit me with some force. Even a neophyte like me could see its potential, and I had to work at hiding my enthusiasm.

"It's a program to help educate kids about space," Charlie explained. "When I left NASA and went home to Oklahoma to help Mama and Daddy when he was dying, I formed my own engineering company. Somehow I also got started lecturing to school kids about America's space program. Soon I was speaking to 10,000 kids a month, and my engineering business took a backseat.

"This became the most absorbing thing I ever did," he told me. "The kids are great. I did all kinds of dangerous testing as an Astronaut Test Crewman and stayed through the *Gemini, Apollo, Skylab,* and *Space Shuttle* programs before Daddy became ill, and young people want to hear about all of them. I wrote several space books for children and helped form the Aerospace Foundation of Oklahoma, because I found there's a tremendous gap in our educational process.

"I sold my engineering company and turned to government contract work so I could help start a space camp for kids. This grew tremendously and became the Space Academy of America, with camp sessions conducted at the Oklahoma City University. I helped lay the foundation, turned it over to competent people, and they have waiting lists today. Youngsters attend camp for two weeks, wear flight suits, learn about space, and even ride in mock-up simulators," he explained.

After glancing through Charlie's materials, I was sold. I admired him not only for himself but also because of his contribution to his country. He had spent several thousand hours in a spacesuit helping train astronauts like Neil Armstrong, the first man to walk on the moon. Part of Charlie's responsibility was simulation missions which would prepare astronauts for being able to walk on the moon and navigate in outer space. I would do all I could to help him find investors and help promote his space programs any way I could. "There's one thing I need to tell you," I began to explain. "I'm moving to Nashville by the first of August, but maybe I could help you some from there."

"Doesn't matter," he said flatly. "My marriage has broken up, and my life is in flux right now. I can come to Nashville just as easily as Atlanta. Maybe I could help you move, if you like. I'd be glad to help you any way I can, Anita Jane."

As it turned out, Charlie did help me move. By then we had made plans for our business venture, and as more time passed we realized we had slipped back into whatever used to draw us together those summers in Tishomingo. Those days he would take me to the movies and want to put his arms around me, but he didn't have the nerve. "I'd count to ten, meaning to put my arm around you then, but you always moved by the time I reached eight or nine, and I'd have to start counting all over again," he confessed. "I was scared to death to put my arm on that seat."

My, that was two score years go. Now we both felt a little wary, somewhat scared. We must take things slowly, we told each other. We weren't kids anymore; probably neither of us could locate the tree where Charlie once carved a heart with our initials inside it. The yellow Jeep was long gone, its riders now middle-aged. We should be cautious, we agreed.

Why, then, did my heart almost burst wide open those times I caught Charlie watching me, smiling that familiar, boyish smile I had known almost forever? I would wait to hear the words I knew Charlie was about to say.

"Anita Jane," he'd begin, in a voice full of wonder, "Do you know that I've loved you for over forty years?"

13
Home to My Roots

*T*he morning of August 19, 1990, the day I would marry Charlie Dry, my Scripture reading included a verse which seemed strikingly appropriate:

"House and riches are the inheritance of fathers: and a prudent wife is from the Lord" (Prov. 19:14).

I read that verse twice, thinking, *Lord, I hope with all my heart I can be that kind of wife to Charlie. That's my intention, with Your help.* But I also thought about the rest of the verse, the part about our earthly inheritance. We had all but depleted ours; Charlie and I had invested a great deal of time and money in our new business venture, and we were nearly broke. Nevertheless, our day dawned bright and splendid in Nashville, Tennessee, that Sunday, and my heart felt as joyous as a thousand pealing bells.

Already our families, friends, and members of the wedding party had begun to arrive, and my usually spacious condominium felt wonderfully crowded. Charlie preempted Bill's room so he could help smooth out some of the chaos, but a constant stream of human traffic flowed through the house. Where's the ironing board? Who is going to church? Where do you want these flowers? Put this with the other gifts.

Sister called to sister, brothers and cousins bantered, and everyone ate, ate, ate. Mama and PawPaw gently tried to keep things moving; I allowed them to take over while I savored the moments.

Within hours, in the sight of God and the people I love most on this earth, I would become Mrs. Charlie Dry. Our wedding would include three ministers of the gospel. Ray McCollum, our Nashville pastor and good friend, would offer a greeting to friends and family with an opening prayer and give us communion as we knelt on our prayer bench. Trudy and Howard Plowman, the Methodist pastor who led Charlie to the Lord during his Oklahoma boyhood, was Charlie's best man and prayed and read Scripture on love—1 Corinthians, chapter thirteen; and my beloved Uncle Luther Berry, a retired Southern Baptist pastor, would perform the ceremony and offer the closing prayer. Charlie's longtime friend Chuck Ivie was to be best man but after arriving, had to leave the following day, when the call came that his ailing mother had passed on into heaven. The joy of our future wedding became tears as we prayed for our friend Chuck and his family.

If ever a wedding had been quickly assembled, this one was planned on unbelievably short notice. Not only did we want it to be small, intimate, and quiet, but it had to be done on a budget. Above all else, however, Charlie and I wanted our ceremony to glorify God. Only the Lord could have planned and perfected our day so magnificently. For one thing, most of our grown children were able to be with us—my elder son and daughter with their wife and husband, my twins and Charlie's daughter Stacy (his other two daughters, Ashley and Charlee, could not attend)—plus a bevy of cousins, my sister Sandra and her husband Sam Page, my beautiful nieces, and more family than I can count. Weeks before in Atlanta, Charlotte Smith gave a lovely luncheon-lingerie shower for me and all my friends. Her chef "Lee" outdid himself. On the huge centerpiece sat a well-dressed stuffed frog. I joked, "I kissed a lot of toads before I met my Prince Charming."

A New Day

The day before the wedding, out-of-town close friends and family were treated to an afternoon pre-rehearsal picnic at the lake home of our dear friends Lanell and Johnny Pageant and also hosted by Molly and Tom Edmondson. It was not your usual type of rehearsal dinner but a lot more fun.

The sultry August day moved forward like a dream . . .100-degree heat . . . flowers somehow dewy fresh . . . our blonde daughters, Gloria, Barbara, and Stacy, beautiful in their chiffon and lacy dresses . . . the men, Bobby, Billy, and son-in-law Bud Sitarz, handsome in dark suits and identical rose-colored neckties . . . Billy, our artist-sculptor, preferring a striped shirt to the plain white everyone else was wearing (I talked him out of it) . . . womenfolk preparing a prewedding meal for kinpeople and other out-of-town guests . . . Mama and my daughters helping me into my blush-pink, Victorian-style wedding dress and a lovely but simple headpiece.

It was almost time. I waited in a room at the rear of the church and chatted with our pastor, Ray McCollum and his wife, Elisabeth. Hope Powell, our photographer, arranged my hands, tilted my chin, snapped some photos. Missy Green had tuned her harp and awaited her part in our ceremony. (When Bobby had married Melissa Lemke, did any of us dream that my son's bride, a professional harpist as well as schoolteacher, would someday perform at his mother's wedding?) I wondered where Charlie was right now . . . what he was thinking and feeling. As for me, despite the swirling activity outside as guests seated themselves and the wedding party took their places, deep peace filled my soul. Happiness, gossamer as the alencon lace on my silky dress, drifted in and out of my thoughts.

Charlie, talking to my parents the previous night, recalled: "Anita's Grandpa Berry would say, 'Guess what? Anita Jane is coming to town.' I'd get a store-bought haircut, and Dad would give me an extra dollar because Anita Jane was coming. She was exceptional, even at that age.

She was strong as a 'goat gut' and definitely superior to the other children."

Standing at the rear of the church, clutching PawPaw's arm, as tears formed in his eyes, I knew he was about to give me to a man who had loved me for as long as either of us could remember. I heard my daughter Barbara and her cousin Melody Crittenden's voices blend in their duet, "I Will Be Here," accompanied by cousin Patsy Crittenden, Uncle Luther's daughter . . . felt, more than heard, the harp's sweet, distinctive sound of "The Lord's Prayer . . . and then, with misty eyes, PawPaw and I began to move, slowly as in a dream sequence, up the aisle towards God's altar, where family and friends would witness the vows Charlie and I offered each other, as unto our Lord.

Step by measured step, I was returning home to my roots. Charlie Dry, the man God gave me, represents the best of all that is good and decent about America. His heritage is my heritage; his speech is my speech; his ideals are my ideals; but above all else, we share the same Almighty God.

We had a perfect wedding, Charlie and I. Our friends waited for us to complete the inevitable photographs and join them at our rather modest, country-club reception. "Any celebrities?" inquired a reporter who showed up. I told him the room was full of them! From years past came a faithful friend and fan who used to write my newsletters, Anne Verrochi and her mom Eva from Brant Rock, Massachusetts. Bob and Gloria Crump and their two young daughters drove from Selma . . . Russell McCraw and Ed Noble and Maria Brown from Atlanta . . . Gordona Duca, now married to Larry Heiliger, traveled from Tulsa . . . Bonnie Brosius, also married now, and her husband Cliff Flood . . . and also from Atlanta, so many friends who had prayed for me during recent years— Karen Finley, Claude and Alice Rodgers, Jim and Alma Davis, Flo and Bill Carroll, our loyal gal Friday, Kellie Porter, and Charlie's cousins Sid and Gerri Goss. Though Dad and Jewel couldn't attend because of their health, my first cousin, O. J. Bray, and his family came from Louisville, Kentucky. My sister Sandra and Sam came with their entire clan, and my nieces, Kathy, Lisa, and Michelle, helped with the guest book and served at the reception. Old friends of Charlie's, Alan and Cathy Stroup, came from Oklahoma with their children.

Those and other friends from far and near, with my large and loyal family, our wonderful kids, and everyone else present, might not have been the *celebrities* the reporter hoped to find, but they are *saints,* people who stuck by me through thick and thin.

Bonnie worked hard to find me a beautiful, affordable wedding dress, and she made my headpiece by hand. Our music was played or sung by various members of my talented family. Gordona insisted on providing punch and a gorgeous wedding cake for our reception, held at the country club of our friends Ken and Kim Brown, as their wedding present. As for a honeymoon, Charlie and I could not take time for that, so our friends Jo Dee and Bill Hoelsher gave us the honeymoon suite at the Opryland Hotel for our wedding night. Mildred Cowen used her talents in arranging the flowers. Yes, we had a "homemade" wedding and reception, and every detail was splendid!

Even my gift to my bridegroom Charlie was something I made by hand and by heart as a special surprise. I wrote and had printed souvenir copies of a poem describing Charlie's life and mine from the first schoolboy-schoolgirl love to the day we married, and I read those verses to him and our guests at the reception. Our friend Brenda Bagel printed it for our wedding present. It is a long poem, too lengthy to quote here, except for the final lines: "No, marriage in Christ doesn't mean you won't have trials and tribulations like other people do. It only means if you love God first, as best friends who love and like each other too, with the Lord's help, you have the power to press on through."

It was a simple poem but heartfelt. As I read those words to my first sweetheart, lifelong friend, and new husband, tears gushed from Charlie's eyes. Sandra presented me a special sister plaque that again brought tears to my eyes.

Our wedding night didn't turn out as expected, for Charlie became deathly ill. We later discovered that most of the wedding party and guests had been contaminated by polluted water in the wedding punch. What a way to start a marriage! Either faith or insanity led us to marry when we did, Charlie and I agreed; certainly, from the standpoint of our circumstances, it made little sense.

My mind reflected back: we had lived in Music City more than a year by then, investing every dollar we could find in our respective business start-ups and Charlie's volunteering many hours speaking in schools. Charlie's Future-Istic Enterprises looked especially promising, but besides his inhumanly long hours of hard labor, he also had to raise big bucks for printing, products, promotion, and other necessities. We came so close to launching Future-Istic Enterprises before funds ran out, and it broke our hearts to put his project on the back burner for a while.

Meanwhile, it looked as though doors were opening for me. I appeared on Ralph Emery's "Nashville Now" several times, interviewed with Crook and Chase and "Entertainment Tonight," helped raise funds for Jerry Rose of Channel 38 in Chicago, sang in Abilene, Texas, for the West Texas Rehabilitation Center Telethon, and signed to co-host the following year. We diligently pursued every lead. We felt sure that God had led us to Nashville and had committed ourselves to hard work, believing that success would follow. We had confidence we would make it!

Months later, we felt much less sure. My prospective deals seemed to hang in limbo, and no amount of prayer or other effort availed. Charlie, unable to find the investors he needed, chafed with inactivity. Despite his big-league engineering background, he could not find even short-term consulting jobs.

"Satan is trying us. We have to dig in and pray harder," I told Charlie.

"We need to decide what to do," he responded with typical practicality. "I am an engineer, and you are a singer. We need to figure out where to go from here. I'm telling you, Anita, it's pretty scary not to have more security at age fifty!"

I didn't like it either. After all, neither of us had been hard up before. After a lifetime of relentless work and high-pressure responsibilities, here we were—apparently helpless, fighting discouragement, but, worst of all, needing supernatural guidance.

"Charlie, we need to get married," I told him.

"What!" he almost shouted at me. "I wouldn't marry you now. I don't have a job, a house, or anything else to give you. I can hardly afford a ring. Why in the world do you think I would ask you to marry me when I can't even pull myself out of the hole?"

"Because we love each other and need to be together," I told him. "We'll get on our feet—you said so yourself. We can do it faster with one dwelling instead of two, by pooling our possessions, our prayers, and our hard work. This is the time, Charlie," I told him calmly. "We're going to fight our way out of this predicament, and we can do it . . . together with the Lord!"

"OK," he said after a moment. "Shall we set the date?" Watching the tension and anxiety on Charlie's face give way to the world's biggest grin, I felt that God, Charlie, and I were in perfect agreement.

Several weeks after our wedding the two of us drove to Oklahoma to visit my folks and take care of some business. On these occasions we usually would visit Charlie's longtime, loyal friends, Sharon and Larry Stinchcomb, or some of my cousins. More and more often, it seemed, we found ourselves heading "home." Dad's chronic illness seemed to be worsening, and Charlie's possessions were stored at his parents' old homestead. Those times we drove to Oklahoma to pick up his computer or visit with the folks, we would both feel that special tug that draws you toward the familiar.

One of our Nashville projects was to be an Anita Bryant Museum. Charlie researched the idea thoroughly and had begun seeking a site. My boxes of irreplaceable memorabilia, including show business, patriotic, and White House mementos, needed a home. Then there were Charlie's trophies, too—his flight suit and shoes, gear worn by various U.S. astronauts on historic space missions, and items of personal recognition for Charlie's contribution to the nation's successful *Apollo II* Mission. As we planned our museum, I began to query family members about our personal heritage. For the first time ever, I felt deep curiosity about my roots.

As we headed back to Nashville after short visits with Dad and Jewel, and with Mother and PawPaw, Charlie and I reminisced about our Oklahoma beginnings. Suddenly, for no reason, he threw an idea my way: "Let's go to Eureka Springs!"

"Where is that?"

"Over in Arkansas . . ."

"Yes, I remember our family driving through there once. Let's go over there!"

Our short tour of the quaint town I half remembered turned into an in-depth, three-day visit. Charlie sensed that the Lord guided us there for a reason, and while I did not quite understand what he meant, I had to admit that this small-town gem exerted a strange pull on me. The neat old houses, peaceful streets and parks, the well-tended flower beds, filled me with nostalgia. Set down among the legendary Ozark Mountains, this town and its friendly occupants seemed like an untroubled plot of pure Americana. The entire city is on the National Register. We immediately felt at home, and we hated to leave.

Charlie likes to explore. He strolled to the Chamber of Commerce to ask some questions, then felt shocked to hear a totally unpremeditated query roll off his lips: "I'm Anita Bryant's husband, and we're thinking of coming here and putting in a theater. Can you tell me some of your demographics?"

"Sure can," replied the gentleman who turned out to be Bob Pervis, the Chamber of Commerce president. "During a six-month period each year, about 1,300,000 people visit Eureka Springs. About half of those come from Oklahoma. About 99 percent of our visitors are Christians who come to see the Great Passion Play."

That sure fits Anita Bryant, Charlie thought. "Anita, something is happening here," he told me. "I don't know what." So we strolled the narrow, winding mountain streets, talked to people, and soaked up the beauty of Eureka Springs. We also saw the Great Passion Play, which the Institute of Outdoor Drama in Chapel Hill, North Carolina, named as the World's Number-One Outdoor Drama.

When Charles Robertson, who heads the Great Passion Play, as well as other related sacred projects on the grounds, and his Executive Director, Bob Foster, invited us to see their reenactment of Jesus Christ's last days of earthly life, I felt certain reservations. Several years earlier I had taken my four children to see the famous Passion Play at Oberammergau, Germany. That was an expensive venture, but I wanted our family to have this once-in-a-lifetime experience. That had been a thrilling day, although the play's spiritual content disappointed me.

Here in the United States, I somehow expected even less of the small-town performance we were about to see. Nothing could have prepared me for the actual event. Some 200 actors, plus live camels, donkeys, horses, sheep, and doves, performed on a multilevel staging area set against the background of a hill called Mount Oberammergau. The reenactment proved so absorbing that at its peak, I couldn't control the tears. I had to agree with Charlie; God had led us here.

When we returned to Nashville, Charlie almost immediately dropped the bombshell. "Anita, I'm going back to Eureka Springs."

"I don't want to move," I came back.

"I don't want to move either, but something is pushing me there," he told me. Within a few weeks, he prepared to leave for the Ozarks. The night before he left, he tossed and turned, unable to sleep. At 3 A.M. Charlie said, "I might as well dress and go." I felt really disturbed but helped him get ready to make his trip.

Then our troubles began. Charlie's car wouldn't start, though he vowed there was nothing wrong with it. During his several attempts to start the automobile, a sudden, violent storm began. "You can't leave in all this thunder and lightning . . ." I began.

"Now I know Old Slewfoot is involved," Charlie muttered. He dropped to his knees and said, "Lord, I'm just a man. You and You alone can open the doors, or please close them." He got into his car, and it started. "Devil, if this is all you can throw at me, I'm going," Charlie said.

About five miles down the road, Charlie told me, he turned on a gospel tape and started to cry like a silly child. Then the tape stopped for no reason. Charlie prayed, "Lord, I will not let the devil stop me." The tape started playing again, and several tapes later he reached Eureka Springs.

The whole scenario seemed strange. Instead of wasting time wondering what was going on, however, I decided to fast and pray. If God were leading Charlie, I could at least back him up with prayer. That night, Charlie phoned to tell me there was a theater for sale in Eureka Springs. The price tag? Three hundred and fifty thousand dollars! I just giggled.

Word had gotten around, Charlie said, and people were coming to him, making offers. "Some of them offered to buy the theater for us, but I'm not making a move," he told me. "I keep asking God, 'Lord, is this what you want us to do?'" I, too, had been praying for God to give us an obvious sign by opening all the doors or closing them.

As my husband's progress reports kept coming, I prayed harder. "Anita, every door is opening for me," he marveled. "All I have to do is walk through. Bankers are showing up at my door, saying, 'Welcome. Do you need anything?' Everyone in town is trying to help us. This is not me; it has to be God."

That week, as Charlie prayed about the theater, the logistics almost effortlessly fell into place. "I know we can make it here, and I think it is from You, but Father, we will need a lot of money," he prayed. Not only did it stagger him to think of buying the theater, but start-up funds, promotion—he could not imagine how to pray. "Please guide me, Lord," he kept asking.

One morning Charles Robertson and Charlie were to meet for breakfast, and Charlie arrived early at the U.S.A.—Four Runners Inn off Highway 62 East near Statue Road, the main entrance to the Passion Play. He found himself charmed that the mother, Fran Runner, and four daughters of the Runners family had bought the place, and began to explore the rooms beyond the dining area as he waited for Charles Robertson to arrive. To his astonishment, there was a convention hall! *We would make this into a theater,* Charlie thought.

Charles Robertson introduced Charlie to the ladies who run the inn, and he asked what they planned to do with the convention space. They would book conventions, they said. Charlie replied that the hall might make a good theater and asked, "What if I brought Anita Bryant here?" They said, "You can't do that." Charlie told them he believed he could, but he would have to have an exceptional deal.

They sat down and worked out a program—the most reasonable terms possible. Charlie told me, "The door opened. The Lord seemed to say, 'You are not going to buy that theater. You are going to start here at the Four Runners Inn and grow, take your time, and let people know that Anita Bryant is here.'"

When Charlie phoned me with the news he said, "The Lord is opening some unbelievable doors. You have a convention hall." Again, I could only giggle and laugh. "What will I do with a convention hall?" I asked him. "I'm going to build you a theater," Charlie said.

That seemed even more preposterous, and again I laughed. The idea of a NASA engineer setting out to build me a theater . . . "You would be impressed if Jones, Jones and Jones, Inc., of New York City were to build your theater," Charlie told me, "but your husband is going to do it." Things were moving too fast to suit me. I prayed even harder.

News from Eureka Springs continued to pour in. Earlier, Charlie had discovered a partially built facility at a good location—actually nothing but footings and foundation work completed—that we could buy very reasonably. *Perfect for our museum,* he thought. That deal already was in the works.

Now he put pencil to paper and began to design a stage with a runway so I could walk out into my audience. That part seemed fairly easy, Charlie said, but when he thought about sound, lighting, and seats, he was keenly aware it would take big bucks. At that juncture, Charles Robertson and Bob Foster at the Great Passion Play saved the day. "I think we have a sound system for you," Mr. Robertson said. When they went to the warehouse to look at it, of course it exactly met the need. It had been in storage for awhile so they gave us a super deal, and we could pay it out.

And so it went. Every time Charlie phoned me with the next mind-blowing report, I laughed. When he returned home and asked me to come back with him to Eureka Springs, though, I did not laugh at all. This was it. I had fasted and prayed for days, trusted God to guide Charlie, prayed that He would make it abundantly obvious to us about what we should do, and now I had cold feet and was upset.

"These are big decisions," I objected. "What if we make a huge mistake?"

"If the Lord Himself opened all those doors for me, how can we fail?" Charlie responded. "What a Partner!"

That was it. I returned to Eureka Springs with Charlie, looked at everything he wanted to show me, and agreed to the move. One big question still remained: Where would we live?

We looked at several houses which did not work for us. Charles Robertson's son Chuck had been checking around for us, and brought us out to Berryville, about fifteen minutes from Eureka Springs, to see a big house on the side of a mountain—one we could not possibly afford, no matter how good the deal. "I know you want it, but I don't know how to pray. We've already asked God for so much!" Charlie said.

I felt there was no way we could have that house. Someone really wanted to sell it, though, and amazingly, we managed to work out a plan. Charlie and I felt absolute awe. It wasn't just the house, however; it was that God provided room for our offices, as well as large living quarters with such amenities as a game room, hot tub, and other comforts. Outside, we had space—a view of the mountainside, clear to the top—and above us on the mountain, a cabin. "You'll have that horse you always wanted, Anita Jane," Charlie promised. He calls those acres Restoration Mountain, because he believes it is part of God's restoration of Anita Jane Bryant.

We did not want to move away from Nashville, so at first we planned to spend six months during the tourist season in Eureka Springs, then the rest of the year in Nashville. I didn't want to move totally and leave our friends and church. It would be difficult, but I insisted that we try. Meanwhile, Charlie sketched plans for extending a high-school stage into a full-fledged theater stage with a runway, drew up a business plan, went to a banker, and obtained a loan. "I designed and built that stage myself— and I'm so proud of it, because I really didn't do it. I don't have the education, training, or capability to build it, but I did," Charlie said. "It was like Noah building the ark. Every day I'd say, 'Lord, I can't do this.' But I did it. I quit every day, prayed every day, and started over every day. I would come home at three in the morning and sleep four hours, then return to the theater."

Besides hours of grueling manual labor, Charlie oversaw a thousand other vital details. Not only did he work night and day to help engineer the sound and light mechanisms, but there were stage curtains to hang, staff to hire, tickets to print. I was swamped with the move, hiring musicians, learning new music, coordinating costumes, props, and staging. I flew to Atlanta for wardrobe fittings with my friend, Bonnie Brosius; sang at Jerri and Pete Pike's (Pike Nurseries) daughter's (Dana's) wedding; then flew to Dallas to co-host the ACTS Network Awards Special, where almost 70 million viewers heard me announce our new show, as well as singing at the wedding of my niece, Lisa Page, to Randy Willard. Had there been time for either of us to stop, we likely might have panicked.

Only as we think through this chapter together, do Charlie and I fully realize the extent of the day-to-day miracles it took for the Lord to lead us from our beloved Nashville to this town so tucked away into the Ozark Mountains that we might never have made a decision to move without God's specific guidance.

When we arrived in Eureka Springs on March 1, 1991, Charles Robertson helped us in more ways than we can enumerate; from the first, he became our prayer partner, confidant, and mentor. As Charlie and I worked harder than we dreamed we could work, it was as though God's people closed in around us. For example, Arlene Foster, my new friend and prayer warrior, had called on her church, Dove Circle Baptist, its pastor Bill Melton, and other church people, like Bob and Flo Cox, to move us into our house. Teams of believers helped cart our belongings up the mountain from the big moving van below, which could not make the steep grade. Others chose, like Jesus, to become servants, scrubbing, polishing, and shining a grand house that had stood empty for seven years. It took much elbow grease to deep clean that house, place our furniture, and unpack our belongings.

"What does all this mean, Lord?" we still ask. Early on, I thought I understood part of the answer when my dad mentioned that my roots go back to Arkansas. Dad's great- grandfather was a full-blooded Indian who served as a scout for the Union Army during the Civil War. Dad's grandfather, Emiziah Bryant, was born in Arkansas, as was his dad, who later married Dorotha Ann Mahan, and moved to Oklahoma in about 1910. "You see, Anita, you and Arkansas go way back," Dad remarked. "You have kinfolks there."

Though Dad's grandfather and father lived in Center Ridge, Arkansas, and I live in Berryville, while working in Eureka Springs, in some deep way I cannot explain, it feels as though at last I have come home to my roots. And yet, God's full plan for Charlie and me continues to unfold. We do not see the entire picture.

Soon after we arrived in Eureka Springs, Charlie mentioned to our new friends, J. B. and Johnell Hunt, that we still could not exactly figure out why we were there. In fact, Charlie confessed, we intended to keep one foot in Nashville until we could see how this enterprise would work out for us.

"I felt exactly the same way," J. B. replied. He had started as a truck driver and now was CEO of a worldwide, billion-dollar trucking firm. "I wanted a test period, too. Then one day the Lord let me know that He wanted me to commit to this place. I had to burn my bridges and not look back."

Those words hit Charlie and me like a hammer blow. We really didn't want to hear it, but we were convinced he was right.

It took a while, but we ultimately came to a decision of total commitment to Eureka Springs.

"We hate to say good-bye to Nashville, but we know God wants us to commit everything we have to Eureka Springs," I told Charles Robertson days later.

"Anita, God brought you here for a reason," he said, his voice sounding very definite. "One of these days I'll tell you why."

14
It's A New Day

On May 18, 1991, the new Anita Bryant Show opened in Eureka Springs, Arkansas!

Backstage, almost up to curtain time, you could hear hammers pound as Charlie and guys like Floyd Clark, Larry Dansforth, and Paul Shaw worked until almost the last minute. Technicians were moving about, musicians testing sound levels and microphones, while I went through my pre-performance routines which over the years almost have become second nature—lyrics, wardrobe, hair, makeup—with my assistant and gal Friday, Beegy Smith, going over last minute-details with me and my dresser, Helaine Dowd.

I felt encircled within a special calm. Despite the ceaseless actions all around me, a core of peace pervaded everything I touched or even thought. I felt those little bubbles of anticipation that come when you are confident you are exactly where you should be, about to do exactly what you should do.

"Lord," I marveled, "we did it!" Charlie actually built me the stage with a ramp to the audience like he said he would. "You sent so much help, Lord, and Charlie really did it!"

Even more amazing was the fact that I actually looked forward to the show. It felt like coming home. I wanted to stand before that audience, communicate with them, and love them through the great songs developed over the years and new ones I truly love to sing. Could this be the same Anita Bryant who said she never wanted to sing again?

Random thoughts pushed into my mind. _God went before us, and we put this theater together with so little money, yet it is complete . . . it isn't perfect, Charlie insisted, but for now it meets our needs._ "Thank You, Lord, for Floyd Clark, Tech Director for The Great Passion Play who, along with Charlie and some others like Larry Dansforth, installed the electrical equipment. Thanks for all the others, including Paul Shaw, too numerous to mention who have helped in so many ways!"

Would we have a good house tonight? "Bless my family and many friends, and Gordona Duca Heiliger, who organized a large group of our Tulsa Will Rogers High School classmates for our gala opening. And thanks to Wayne Campbell, my longtime pianist-conductor, who helped me find excellent musicians to produce the high-quality sound our show requires."

I had prayed continually for the Lord to send the right people personally and professionally. Our drummer Dexter Greene, originally from Chicago, came from college in Annapolis, Maryland, after I sent a letter to the school asking that Dexter be allowed to come in time for the opening and take his exams in Arkansas. Buddy Harmon, drummer on the Grand Ole Opry in Nashville, and married to my cousin Marsha, helped me find bass guitarist Kirby Hoffman, also a Will Rogers graduate from Tulsa. My old friend and arranger Bill Purcell, now a professor at Belmont College, Nashville, recommended his top student, Jonathan O'Kain, from McMinnville, Tennessee, as our keyboard player. Jonathan was a graduate student working in arranging and also doing backup singing. Jonathan mentioned his roommate Keith Wood, from Mena, Arkansas (not on the map), who played trumpet and also sang. I hired him immediately when I learned he was taught by my old friend Don (Jake) Jacobe, who played trumpet when I was the girl singer on the famed radio show "Don McNeill's Breakfast Club." Our guitar player, Bob Scrogham, born in Fort Worth, Texas, now from Fayetteville, Arkansas, had spent most of his career in Los Angeles and had played for Bob Hope.

As showtime approached, Charlie, Charles Robertson, Bob and Arlene Foster, Wayne, and the other musicians, "Anita's Band Boys" as I called them, gathered around for prayer and praise. How we thanked God for His mercies and praised Him for what He was about to do!

Then came the glad sounds of our band's musical overture, then my intro music began, the curtains parted, and I was on. More than 600 people had crowded into our theater! Their applause filled the house with energy. We did all my best numbers, a medley of my earliest hit recordings, fast costume changes into the country-and-western segment that makes audiences laugh and stomp, a 50s medley of oldie-goodies, with me doing the twist and jitterbugging with someone in the audience, a new song called "Men," several romantic, big-band pieces, then the exciting set of upbeat numbers from "That's Entertainment," where I moved all over the stage and down the ramp, with rainbow lights following and plenty of lush orchestral sounds.

The second half of our show celebrated God and our country. I marched in from the front of the theater twirling a baton, decked out in a sequined majorette costume I had preserved from a show in the 60s. We opened with our National Anthem and progressed into an upbeat gospel medley and some sacred music, including my song "I Am What I Am," along with sharing my testimony for the Lord, and perennial favorites most Americans never tire of hearing: "Amazing Grace," "How Great Thou Art," "God Bless America," and others in that vein—and closing with the mighty "Battle Hymn of the Republic."

Word on the street had it that protesters would picket us on opening night. "I spent a lot of my borrowed money hiring security. I was afraid for Anita," Charlie explained to some friends. "I have a shield around me," I told him. "Don't worry, there are many people praying, and the Lord will protect us." No protesters appeared. As a matter of fact, many gays saw the show and not only loved it but recommended it to their friends.

It was called a beautiful performance, thank God, and tired as we were, Charlie and I, along with our staff, felt pure joy and elation. After the show, family and friends crowded around and welcomed us. Despite all the problems we still faced, that night Charlie and I knew—we deeply believed—that our miraculous, homemade theater was meant to exist. The Lord intended for me to perform on the stage Charlie built for me.

People continued to come, many by the busload, night after night, week after week, throughout the Eureka Springs "season." Old friends arrived. Charlie's friend Billy Williamson worked tirelessly to film our show for later video release. Even family members who have heard me sing all my life traveled to catch my "new" show, which features more than two hours of the most popular music I ever sang or recorded. Cousins Gee Gee and Derrell Spears, along with Uncle Luther and Aunt Marie, came to the opening with their granddaughter Julie Berry, and Patsy Crittenden with her husband Wendall. They loved the show so much both the Berrys and Crittendens came back to see it later with a busload of their friends. My niece Kathy Odom and her husband Joey also organized a busload from their church, First Methodist in Marshall, Texas.

Reviews of the show were excellent. With regular income once more, Charlie and I began to catch up with ourselves financially. Many weeks ahead I trained hard physically and vocally, ate right, and spent a lot of quiet time with Jesus to prepare for the season. The six-shows-a-week routine was strenuous, particularly when an outside booking stretched it to seven days, but the Lord provided both of us strength as we needed it.

"It's a new day!" people exclaimed, and we believed them.

One of the best aspects about our life, Charlie and I told each other, was how our new friends and neighbors had involved themselves with our project and worked, helped, and prayed for us. Charles Robertson, for example, always met me in the lobby after each performance. His encouragement to Charlie and me never has wavered. His is the kind of old-fashioned Christian friendship that means everything.

With Charles, who is an ordained minister, Charlie and I minister to those individuals who always seek us out for prayer. Our program's message—that of God's being our help—encourages that man or woman fighting cancer, facing heart surgery, or troubled about anything at all, to ask us for prayer. From the outset, our theater has seemed like holy ground. God meets with us there every night.

Although at first we had no time or big budget for advertising our show, Eureka Springs is the kind of town where one enterprise helps another, and we soon realized that our neighbors were passing the word along to tourists. Also, like other tourist communities, there are always certain persons who will go to any lengths to keep out competition. The Anita Bryant Show prospered from the beginning, thanks to our loving God and our caring neighbors.

But if God chose one single person to serve as a standard bearer for Charlie and me, that man is Charles Robertson. Still vigorous and energetic in his seventies, Charles, perhaps more than any other person I know, exemplifies the enormous visionary power available to the person who follows God's directions and does not hesitate to launch "impossible" projects.

Charles Robertson entered our lives at precisely the right moment. It seemed impressive enough to Charlie and me that he as President manages The Great Passion Play. What I did not realize, however, was that God had used Charles to *create* that spectacular and majestic drama, as well as several other related sacred projects. This unpretentious Christian servant, it turned out, had pioneered some monumental efforts, usually proceeding with no foreseeable funding but acting entirely on God's say-so.

Charlie and I wanted to know more about this kind of godly success. "He doesn't look like a daring entrepreneur," my husband remarked, "yet this is one of the most creative businessmen I ever met, also a fine preacher!"

"He *uses* his talents in the Lord's service," I replied. "Yet with all his success, Charles Robertson is one of the most truly humble personalities I ever met. He is a wonderful Christian model for us, Charlie."

Our quiet, unassuming "model" continued to help us and serve as our mentor, and Charlie and I have loved him from the beginning. His kind of friendship gives everything and asks for nothing. We learned that Charles F. Robertson came to Eureka Springs in 1964 on behalf of the well-known evangelist and speaker Gerald Smith and his wife, Elna. The Smiths settled here and, at the age when most people retire, began to sell their earthly possessions and create the shrines which would remind visitors of God's great gift to mankind on the cross of Calvary. Jesus said, ". . . and if I be lifted up, I will draw all men unto me."

The Smiths bought Magnetic Mountain and determined to erect a huge statue of Christ upon its summit. Charles Robertson described the day Mr. Smith drew an X on the ground with the toe of his shoe and said, "Charles, you are going to build a seven-story-tall statue of Jesus Christ right here."

The idea had gestated in the mind of one man for years, until that moment in 1964 when it burst forth. Where would they find a sculptor? How would they pay for the mammoth undertaking? As Charlie and I listened in fascination, we learned more about the "drama behind the drama," and about Charles Robertson, the extraordinary but ordinary man who, there in a typical mid-American vacation resort town, built something more far-reaching than most people's dreams can ever encompass. How did he do it?

Charles related that their research revealed the two most qualified sculptors for the job could be found in Rio de Janeiro . . . or in Eureka Springs! The latter, a man named Emmet Sullivan, had worked on the famous Mount Rushmore carvings and "just happened" to be vacationing in Eureka Springs. Smith commissioned him to sculpt what today is known worldwide as the "Christ of the Ozarks," completed in 1966. Robertson had managed and facilitated that work, for which it seemed there were no funds.

Gazing at the commanding "Christ of the Ozarks" statue and building our new beginnings almost literally in the shadow of that Presence, how could Charlie and I not believe God would guide our efforts? And as we listened to the spellbinding details of how God used Charles Robertson to help fulfill this vision, we felt grateful that Charles's ministry of helps also extended to us.

Where did the men find the funds needed to construct the gigantic statue? There was no bank account, so they looked at Smith's possessions to see what could be sold. In surveying the items Smith, a discerning collector, had accumulated through the years during his travels, they discovered not only precious items that could be sold to fund the statue, but literally hundreds of fine paintings depicting Jesus Christ and numerous museum-quality Bibles as well. Some rare copies of the Holy Bible belonging to Smith dated back to A.D. 900 and A.D. 1100. Those two collections became the nucleus of what now is the Sacred Arts Center and the Bible Museum, which draws scholars from all over the world.

Through the ensuing years, the Smith and Robertson vision grew ever larger. The aging evangelist told Charles,

"I am bequeathing you enough work for the next forty years." Robertson, knowing they had no funds for the work, asked, "Lord, what am I going to do?" This part of the story reminds me of Jack McDowell's lesson to me: "Anita, God will build your future from the foundation of what He already has given you in the past."

I thought of Smith's unique Bibles, identified by the University of Heidelberg as among the sixty most important Bibles in existence. I knew Smith could not have dreamed of their rarity as he acquired them, one by one.

Emmet Sullivan, sculptor in charge of the Christ of the Ozarks work, was eighty years old when he began the exacting project, but could still climb the scaffolding ropes hand over hand. He chose Adrian Forrett as his associate so the statue could be completed in the event of his death. Forrett, a man in his fifties, heard that Smith's next project was to be creating a passion play. "My best friend is a writer and says his life's work will not be fulfilled until he writes a passion play!" the sculptor exclaimed. That is how the script for The Great Passion Play came into being, and how God led them—and leads us—one step at a time.

During 1966 and 1967 Robertson not only commissioned and oversaw the Passion Play script but began carving a multilevel amphitheater on the 167-acre mountainside. He gathered a cast of performers and supervised the drama's production. The sacred reenactment opened in July 1968 to worldwide notice. The press, awed by its scope, insisted that the word "Great" be incorporated into its title.

Prior to Smith's death in 1976, Robertson constructed the 1975 addition to the complex, the Smith Memorial Chapel. The aging saint had left Robertson a verbal plan for the New Holy Land he envisioned, to be established on the Elna M. Smith Foundation grounds, with a list of thirty sites significant to the life of Christ which must be situated there. To date, Robertson has not only prepared the New

Holy Land, but also established the Christ of the Ozarks statue, the Great Passion Play amphitheater, the Sacred Arts Center, the Church in the Grove, the Smith Memorial Chapel, the Bible Museum, the Great Wall (Eastern Gate), and several other functional additions as well.

Charlie and I studied this massive creation more than once, awed at the imaginative and powerful vision, not to mention the practical and artistic skills, of two men who truly allowed God to lead them into monumental exploits. What would God teach us through the work of these men? I felt sure there would be something specific for us to learn.

Today, Robertson shares his continuing vision with us. Many of the thirty sites within the New Holy Land remain to be constructed, yet this does not trouble him. More than three years ago, he told us, God assured him He would send someone to help with the work. A true culmination of the New Holy Land, however, must begin soon, and a great amount of financial help will be necessary. Robertson intends to build the temple which will be based on Zerubbabel's measurements of the original temple and a type and shadow of the temple in heaven, proclaiming the judgments of Revelation to bring people to repentance and faith in Christ. As he dreams aloud of that project with Charlie and me, my mind parallels his words . . .

Author of a magnificent life's work, I thought, *a godly man continues to dream, undismayed by the fact that he may not live to see his dream become a completed reality.* Smith could trust his beloved confidant, Robertson, to carry on the work he first envisioned, then began. As Charlie said about God, "What a partner!"

Doesn't Robertson's attitude toward his life's work reflect God's attitudes and plans for the human family? I wondered. We begin a family by faith, not knowing how long our life may last or where it may take us. How crushed I felt when I believed I had failed my parents and children! How we grieve for those children, when we fear we cannot provide even their needs, much less their desires.

Smith and Robertson could grieve for their own uncompleted vision, I thought, *except that they placed their life's hard work and fondest dream upon the altar of God. Had I truly done the same with my children?*

I had to chuckle, remembering the tears I shed the day Bobby left for college. At Wheaton College, Bobby met Melissa Lemke, his future bride, the woman I believe God chose for my son. Talented, handsome, and old-fashioned "nice," those two share so many common interests. Bobby likes literature, journalism, and history, while Melissa enjoys teaching and playing the harp, among other pursuits. Both love to travel. Both are sold out to the Lord.

Then there's my sweet, serious Gloria, whom Russell McCraw calls "The Pearl Girl." He considers her almost exactly what a young Christian woman should be, and most of the time, I agree. (Sorry, Gloria, but I know you aren't perfect.) Gloria graduated from Oral Roberts University, where she met her future husband, "Bud" Hans-Walter Sitarz, Jr. Gloria prepared herself for social work, receiving her master's degree this past year, and now works in a medical center at Beaver, Pennsylvania, a suburb of Pittsburgh. Bud chose a career in international banking and is now an international banking officer at Pittsburgh National Bank. They purchased their first home this past spring. Bud is as dear to me as my own sons, and observing their old-fashioned courtship was like going back in times past. I recalled the day I cried because I couldn't afford the wedding dress Gloria wanted, but she stayed unflappable. "If the Lord wants me to have it, Mom, there will be a way," she consoled. As it turned out, there was.

The twins? I have put them on the altar time and again, from the day they were born. These were my miracle babies, so tiny at birth, Billy weighing 2 lbs. 12 oz. and Barbara, 2 lbs. 10 oz., that it was weeks before doctors felt sure they would make it. Boy and girl twins, of course, are non-identical; these two individualists from day one scrapped, competed, and asserted themselves. They love each other dearly and, praise God, now have become mature enough to admit it. Bill soon will graduate from the Pratt Institute in New York City; Barbara will graduate from Birmingham Southern with an English major. She is my singer, while Bill majored in fine arts as a sculptor.

Had I placed these children on the altar? *Yes,* I decided, *I know I did.* There is no other choice. I believe each one is rooted and grounded in his or her faith. God will take care of the outcome. He cares for His own.

Like the New Holy Land and the building of the temple Charles Robertson still works to complete, I realized my life is still under construction. It will not be completed here, but I can trust God for its eventual outcome!

It was a new day for my dad. We planned to visit him that weekend, Charlie and I, because Dad was sicker, and I wanted to spend every moment with him that I could. God had restored my father and me to each other, and Dad had done much to restore me to my own heritage.

Before our anticipated visit, however, the call came. My brother Sonny telephoned me at 3 in the morning. I had been restless and unable to sleep, for some reason, so I decided to try to relax in the hot tub. Now I knew why God had wakened me.

Just before the phone call, I saw Dad in my mind. He seemed the picture of health, radiant and smiling. Jesus was standing at the foot of Dad's bed . . . and my father was the happiest I've ever seen him as he leaped up from bed to join Jesus! That mental picture had not seemed like a premonition, but as a joyous gift from God. For weeks I had prayed for God to heal my father or take him home. He hated to be bedfast.

Now I tried to comfort Sonny. "Remember what our

dad told you the other day," I said. "I'm not passing on . . . I'm just going on down the road, and I'll see you in a little while."

The next day, I dug, planted, and worked in our garden all day, alone and at peace. It was a radiant early-August day, all green and gold, with no sign of a breeze. As I worked and thought, a song began coming to me, "I'm just going on down the road, and I'll see you in a little while. . . ."

Dad's words to Sonny! More words, more music, as I continued to water my garden. My heart felt peaceful and still as the air. Then it happened: Three bell tones sounded, deliberate and perfect as the three tones which precede the opening bars of the "Battle Hymn of the Republic." The tones sounded soft and clear. I turned toward the old, but newly restored, wind chimes which hung nearby, and my heart jumped as I instinctively whispered, "Daddy?"

That was all. The chimes in our yard were long and heavy; they would have produced a loud tone. There was no breeze, nothing to disturb that chime. But I heard it, gentle as a whisper from father to child.

I sang at my father's services. Rev. George Jesse, who pastors the Indian church outside Sasakawa and, like Dad, mostly Native American, preached. I sang "How Great Thou Art."

At the Oakwood Cemetery between Wewoka and Sasakawa, where all the Bryants are laid to rest, I sang "Amazing Grace." It seemed as though I sang it especially to Sonny.

"How did you do it?" he asked me. "That was beautiful."

"I could not do that myself, Sonny, "I answered. "Only God could make it possible."

It *is* a new day. God, whose mercies are new every morning, woke me recently with a call from Jewel. My brother Sonny has given his life to the Lord, as has his wife Monica and son Monty, and they have begun attending church with their two young children. "This is an answer to years of prayer," Sonny's mother, Jewel, explained.

Charlie and I look ahead with high hopes and confidence. We're learning about our town . . . the amazing numbers of Christian ministers and evangelists who have come here through the years . . . and the prophecy, attributed to Corrie ten Boom and Maria von Trapp, who saw legions of angels with drawn swords doing battle in the heavenlies over this part of the Ozarks.

I think of Mr. Robertson's belief that Eureka Springs eventually will become America's gospel-music capital. And I recall, again and again, how God led Charlie to this place and how He made me willing to follow him here.

"What did you mean to tell me about God's plans for Eureka Springs?" I asked Charles Robertson the other day. "You said God told you He would send someone . . ."

"You are that person, Anita," Charles Robertson replied. I felt totally astounded. "Are you sure?"

The great man we so admire did not hesitate. "I knew it the evening we met," he explained. "The Lord told me to do everything I could to help you come here."

Your new day begins when you arrive at the place God intends. This world promises little beyond struggle; God's promises are yea and amen. I think of that verse of "Amazing Grace," the hymn so many of us love:

> "Through many dangers, toils, and snares
> I have already come;
> 'Tis grace that bro't me safe thus far,
> And grace will lead me home."

Amen and Amen!